PACKING AND MOVING TIPS THAT COULD SAVE YOU A FORTUNE

PACKING AND MOVING TIPS THAT COULD SAVE YOU A FORTUNE

John Marc

This text refers to the care and handling of household goods only and in no way offers any recommendation, advice or instruction regarding the operation of the vehicle, the towing of any vehicle, Or the loading and transport of any item outside the confines of the van.

Copyright © 1997, 2000 by John Marc

All rights reserved.
No part of this book may be reproduced, stored in a retrieval system, or transmitted by any means, electronic, mechanical, photocopying, recording, or otherwise, without written permission from the author.

ISBN: 1-58820-539-8

The Publisher and Author disclaims any personal liability, loss, or risk as a consequence of the use and application, either directly or indirectly of any advice, information, or methods contained herein.

This book is printed on acid free paper.

1stBooks - rev. 11/15/00

This Publication is dedicated to the guys who taught me the basics
and to all who have ever trusted me
with their belongings

TABLE OF CONTENTS

CHAPTER ONE

    Introduction 1

CHAPTER TWO

    Did You Rent A Big Enough Truck?... 4

CHAPTER THREE

    Professional Services 6

CHAPTER FOUR

    Packing Materials.. 8

        Dish pack
        Small carton
        Medium carton
        Large carton
        Extra large carton
        Wardrobe
        Picture carton
        Original carton
        Professional vs. supermarket
        News print paper
        Paper pad
        Bubble wrap
        Tape
        Shrink wrap

CHAPTER FIVE

    Discard And Measure 14

CHAPTER SIX

    Items Not To Pack.. 16

CHAPTER SEVEN

    Should This Item Be Packed? 20

CHAPTER EIGHT

How To Fold And Tape A Carton 22

CHAPTER NINE

Overall Recommendations 26

CHAPTER TEN

Packing Furniture 28

CHAPTER ELEVEN

Pack Last 30

CHAPTER TWELVE

My Way 32

CHAPTER THIRTEEN

Pack First 34

    Books
    Records and Albums
    Videos
    Cassettes
    Discs
    Air shipping disks
    Stereos and Components
    Speakers
    Wiring
    Pictures-Mirrors (illustrations)
    Telescope packing (illustrations)
    Flat Glass (no frame)
    Marble-glass table tops
    Bulletin Boards

CHAPTER FOURTEEN

Kitchen Items 40

    Can goods
    Bottles-jar foods
    Box foods-spices
    Cleaning items (under the sink)
    Small appliances

    Pots and pans
    Silverware-junk drawer-sharp knives
    Dishes
    Silver

CHAPTER FIFTEEN

Lamps **44**

    Shades
    Dry run-lamp shades
    Floral arrangements

CHAPTER SIXTEEN

Capping **48**

    Illustrations

CHAPTER SEVENTEEN

Computers **52**

CHAPTER EIGHTEEN

Linens **54**

CHAPTER NINETEEN

Bathroom Items **56**

CHAPTER TWENTY

Closet Items **58**

    Clothing
    Shoes-purses
    Hats
    Neckties
    Belts

CHAPTER TWENTY ONE

Jewelry **62**

    Coins
    Wedding gifts

CHAPTER TWENTY TWO

Toys 64

    Games
    Doll houses

CHAPTER TWENTY THREE

Fixtures 68

    Drapes- blinds
    Chandeliers
    Ceiling fan

CHAPTER TWENTY FOUR

Sewing Machines 70

CHAPTER TWENTY FIVE

Grandfather Clock 72

CHAPTER TWENTY SIX

Throw Rugs 74

CHAPTER TWENTY SEVEN

Piano Bench And Music 76

CHAPTER TWENTY EIGHT

Weapons 78

    Ammunition

CHAPTER TWENTY NINE

Fireplace Items 80

CHAPTER THIRTY

Long Items 82

CHAPTER THIRTY ONE

Mattresses 84

CHAPTER THIRTY TWO

Patio Item 86

    Patio tables
    Flower Pots
    Concrete
    Fountains
    Bricks and concrete blocks

CHAPTER THIRTY THREE

Garage Items..88

    Weights

CHAPTER THIRTY FOUR

Be Prepared 92

CHAPTER THIRTY FIVE

Disassemble 94

    Keys
    China cabinet or hutch
    Dining and kitchen table
    Shrink wrapping leather or vinyl
    Shrink wrap upholstery (illustration)
    Recliner
    Hide-a-bed (illustration)
    Trundle bed or Hollywood
    Exercise equipment
    Ironing board
    Headboard
    Bed frames
    Crib and play pen
    Toddler items
    Armoire
    Drafting table
    Desk
    Shelves
    Coffee-end tables
    Curio cabinet-glass case
    Entertainment center
    Small stereo cabinet
    Tiered glass bookcase
    Electrical cords

Built-ins
Refrigerator-freezer food
Microwave oven
Washer
Dryer
Air condition-humidifier
Playhouse-castle-cabin, etc.
Swing set
Barbecue
Garden hose
Table saw-machinery
Bicycles
Fuel burning lawn equipment
Greasy-oily items

CHAPTER THIRTY SIX

Appliance Dolly 104

Furniture pads

CHAPTER THIRTY SEVEN

Loading The Truck 106

ILLUSTRATION #1
ILLUSTRATION # 2
ILLUSTRATION # 3
ILLUSTRATION # 4

CHAPTER THIRTY EIGHT

Furniture Handling 114

Long items
Sliding appliance
Bulky sofa
Mattress-overhead 115

CHAPTER THIRTY NINE

Pianos 118

Words to the wise
Stairs
Grand piano-stairs

CHAPTER FORTY

Load A Previously Damaged Item **122**

    Illustration #1
    Illustration #2

CHAPTER FORTY ONE

Self Storage **126**

CHAPTER FORTY TWO

Cold Weather **128**

CHAPTER FORTY THREE

Keep Packing Materials **130**

INTRODUCTION

CHAPTER ONE

This Publication is the culmination of over twenty years of tried and tested methods in the professional moving industry. It is designed as an aid in the completion of a moving task with the least amount, if any, of property, packing, and household goods damage, as well as bodily injury.

The author of this Publication has served more than two decades as a professional operator in the household goods moving industry with such carriers as Mayflower, Global, Allied, North American, and Suddath/United Van Lines.

Whether your move be local, short, or long distance, the task can be a traumatic experience. The information contained herein can remove much of that trauma and save you money.

This Publication covers a gamut of steps necessary to complete your project whether it be the entire move, packing your own items for carrier transport, or simply storing your goods.

Read the booklet from cover to cover, follow the guidelines, and refer back to each step and illustration as you go. The outcome should be a successful, damage-free move.

DID YOU RENT A BIG ENOUGH TRUCK?

CHAPTER TWO

DID YOU RENT A BIG ENOUGH TRUCK?

I have a legitimate reason for asking this question. Let me explain. I cannot tell you how often I have arrived at someone's home with the intention of moving the estimated amount of household goods. Let's use five thousand pounds as an example. I tour the home and discover that the job consists upwards of seven thousand pounds.

Once the discussion with my customer is opened, I invariably hear the words, "How can that be? The weight was only five thousand when we moved in three years ago, and we haven't bought anything."

Loosely interpreted, my customer is telling me that he or she hasn't purchased any major items. However, everyone buys something almost every day. We are a race of people born to accumulate........... books, pictures, knick knacks, clothing, linens, videos, sports equipment, bikes, etc. The list goes on.

Every single item weighs something, however slight. The sum of all these items can easily equal (in this example) two thousand pounds. That extra two thousand pounds will inevitably take up more space.

At least with a rental truck you have an option. Chances are the truck you rented will have a trailer hitch. If not everything fits inside the truck, perhaps an additional trailer will solve your problem.

This is one option the professionals don't have.

PROFESSIONAL SERVICES

CHAPTER THREE

PROFESSIONAL SERVICES

If, for whatever reason, you find yourself in need of someone to help with all or any part of your move, there are services available from many sources that are geared to handle any problem.

Your truck rental agency or local moving company can certainly help you with various packing materials and equipment.

Most moving companies can furnish contract labor to load and unload the truck and also to pack and unpack your furnishings.

Heavy equipment and piano services are also only a phone call away. Your local moving agency can also help with what we call "third party" services.... people that come to your home to crate specified items on the spot, service clocks, major appliances, remove chandeliers, dismantle drapery rods, etc. Costs may vary, but estimates are usually free of charge.

I, for one, use contract labor consistently to help me load and unload most all shipments.

PACKING MATERIALS

CHAPTER FOUR

PACKING MATERIALS

The following is an outline of various sized cartons and accompanying materials required to successfully pack your household goods.

Dish pack
 - 18" x 18" x 27", Load Capacity 5.1 cu.ft., Gross Wt. 100 lbs.

The dish pack is the superman of packing cartons. It is entrusted with the utmost care and protection for your dishes, glassware, lamps, pictures, knick knacks, and anything else breakable. It's the only carton that can handle heavy weight and yet protect your most delicate fragile items.

It is also the most expensive, but well worth the price. Given the opportunity, the choice, and the budget, I, for one, would pack everything I own in a dish pack.

Small carton
 - 16 1/2" x 12 3/4" x 12 3/4", Load Capacity 1.5 cu.ft., Gross Wt. 70 lbs.

This carton can handle books, papers, files, records, albums, disks, cassettes, videos, can goods, bottles, jars, bricks, and weights. Almost all small heavy items.

Medium carton
 - 18 1/2" x 18" x 16", Load Capacity 3.0 cu.ft., Gross Wt. 30 lbs.

This carton can hold the bulk of your belongings, such as: shoes, purses, hats, folded clothing, linens, small pictures, knick knacks, lamps and shades, small appliances, box foods, Tupperware, plastics, pots and pans, toys, games, photos, albums, silverware, cooking utensils, small tools, cleaning supplies, bath items, cosmetics, artificial flowers, and the like.

Large carton
 - 18" x 18" x 24", Load Capacity 4.5 cu.ft., Gross Wt. 25-40 lbs.

This carton usually accommodates bedding, closet items, folded clothing, toys, and any item too large for the medium carton. This carton is also great for fairly large paintings or pictures (without any glass) which you can stand on end against the flat surfaced sides of the carton.

Extra large carton
 - 24" x 18" x 24", Capacity 6.0 cu.ft., Gross Wt. 30 lbs.

Don't let the size of this carton fool you. Although it is the largest of the group, it is quite limited as to the weight it can hold. (Note again the estimated gross weight) Large, light items such as lamp shades, artificial plants, quilts, pillows and cushions, or plastics are about all one should pack in these giants.

I have seen these cartons crammed with books, tools, canned goods, and other heavy objects that have caused the carton to weigh upwards of 90-100 lbs. Consequently, bottoms give way, sides blow out, corners split, and major damage in broken, soiled, crushed, or lost items occurs.

I realize the temptation is great, but the cost in damage could be much greater.

Wardrobe,
from 18" to 22" wide, Gross Wt. 40 lbs.

This carton is for hanging clothing or drapes only. Don't be tempted to load the bottom, This could result in a large cleaning bill.

When packing a wardrobe, pack it tightly. The clothing and hangers are less apt to fall from the bar and end up scrunched on the wardrobe bottom.

Picture carton
- Maximum Gross Wt. 80 lbs.

When shopping for this carton, be sure to ask for the section type picture carton. They are no more expensive than the single piece, yet much more practical. Use of the sections will enable you to fit the carton tightly around any size picture, mirror, or painting that needs packing.

Original carton

Stereo, TV, and electronic cartons are ideal to reuse if you've saved them, provided you can solve the riddle of the foam framework.

Professional vs. supermarket

It's a widely known fact that one of the first items on the agenda to save a few bucks in preparing for a move is a planned raid on those huge dumpsters behind the local supermarkets for packing boxes. Over the years, I've found that to be penny-wise and pound-foolish!

To begin with, it's very difficult to find a market box with the lid still intact. Consequently, the odds are high that much of the contents will be broken, crushed, or lost. If you find your budget a bit too tight for new moving cartons, shop around for used ones. Almost everyone in the moving business stocks perfectly good used cartons at very reasonable prices.

News print pager

I would not advise wrapping any item in printed newspaper. I have seen devastating results from printers' ink that had penetrated fine china, glassware, and porcelain pieces. I'm certain your rental agency or local moving company will stock this item.

Paper pad

This 5' x 6' item compliments the family of packing materials in many ways. It consists of two outer sheets of brown paper with an inner sheet of thick corrugated paper, perfect for wrapping stereo equipment, electronics, extra large dishes, flower pots, pictures, mirrors, glass shelves, and even small pieces of furniture, such as jewelry boxes, music boxes, statues, lamps, and anything of that nature.

It's a vital necessity if your inventory consists of any of the above. If used properly, paper pads could also replace many of the rental pads you'll need from the rental agency. They can also be reused over and over again for storing items in garages or storage areas. It's most definitely a money saving item. You'll be reading more about the paper pad in the remaining segments.

Bubble wrap

For you electronic buffs who feel a bit uncomfortable wrapping your highly prized computers in paper, I would suggest 'bubble wrap'.

Bubble wrap is a sheet of transparent plastic material full of small round pockets of air bubbles.

Many of the pros use it, primarily in office moves for wrapping typewriters, electronics, and various other office machines.

It's great, but it's expensive. However, you might check the cost before you make the decision. Availability and prices do vary.

Tape

When packing your items in cartons that will weigh anywhere from ten to a hundred pounds, it's important to use strong tape, industrial strength, if you will; Scotch or masking tape will never do. Just about all the household goods carriers use plastic tape. It comes in gray, brown, or transparent colors. It's almost impossible to break with your fingers, and it adheres very well. Your rental company is sure to have it in stock

Shrink wrap

If at all possible, while you're stocking up on packing materials, beg, borrow, or buy a roll or two of 'shrink wrap'. Otherwise known as 'stretch film' or glorified industrial strength 'saran wrap', a name you homemakers are familiar with.

Everyone seems to have their own terminology for this item. Don't ask where they got the name 'shrink wrap', but it's the term I'm most familiar with so I'll stick with it throughout this text. I can assure you that nothing that has been wrapped in this stuff has ever shrunk.

Transparent, and in roll form, it has become a godsend for me, a vital tool in the prevention of damage with respect to household goods. For years, it has been widely used by manufacturers for the transportation of pallets stacked with various cartons to prevent spillage and toppling.

Several years ago, this system was adopted by many of the household goods carriers for use in the prevention of upholstery damage. Some of us in the business have taken shrink-wrapping quite a few steps further. I am one of those people.

I have read reports from various carriers that shrink-wrapping has cut upholstery damage claims up to eighty percent. Not one to hurriedly welcome change, I was hesitant about using this film. I actually hated it....for about ten minutes, the length of time it took for me to learn how to apply it.

It adheres to itself, thereby eliminating the use of tape. It seems to aid in gripping such bulky items as a sofa. It has simplified the tedious job of padding a sofa and cut the number of pads tremendously.

As you read on, you'll find the many other uses I have discovered for this too. Follow the guidelines and illustrations, and spend the few minutes it takes to apply this film. It will save you time in loading, make handling easier, and save you money. Most moving companies stock this fine item. Retail costs may vary. Whatever the cost, I can assure you that it's worth every penny.

DISCARD AND MEASURE

CHAPTER FIVE

DISCARD AND MEASURE

Discard

Throughout my career, I have discovered that a great number of people spend time and effort to move certain items that should be discarded, donated, or sold prior to the move. I'm referring to items that have simply outlived their usefulness, items that they knew wouldn't fit in the new residence, or items that he or she just couldn't part with. Moving these items can cost you labor, space in the truck, and the cost of packing materials.

Many of us hate to give up these choice items that have over the years become so dear to our hearts...the rickety old wood chair with the loose legs and the broken arm, the spindly lamp table with the top stained and the finish all but worn off, or the old chest or dresser with the missing caster and stuck drawers. Those items that you suspect will spend the rest of eternity taking up space and gathering dust in your garage or storage area will cost you money.

Measure

And finally, will your ten by ten living room accommodate your sixteen foot, five hundred pound, high-backed, triple recliner, hide-a-bed sofa?

If you don't know, I beg of you...have mercy on yourself!. Find out for sure, before you attempt to fight that monster.

ITEMS NOT TO PACK

CHAPTER SIX

ITEMS NOT TO PACK

It's very difficult to choose what items to discard. Even items not considered hazardous by themselves can react with certain other items that could still cause you problems.

First and foremost, don't pack any other container that's labeled hazardous, corrosive, or reactive.

The following is a list provided to our customers and us by the Household Goods Carriers.

Combustible Liquids:	Alcohol Antifreeze compounds Camphor oil Disinfectants Type cleaners(fluids containing combustible Material, i.e. spot cleaners, office machine liquid Cleaners, etc.)
Corrosive Liquids:	Acids, photographic, used in developing film Etching ink Iron/steel rust preventing compounds Psoriatic acid Sulfuric acid
Explosives:	Black powder Cigarette loads Dynamite, plastic or similar explosives Explosive auto alarms Explosive flash bulbs Fireworks
Explosives (cont.):	Small arms ammunition (see Note 1) Primers Smokeless powder Souvenir explosive instruments of war Spear guns having a charged head Toy propellant or smoke devices Brick matches Brick noise makers (firecrackers) Flammables: Adhesives (glues, cements, plastics) Aerosol cans (flammable contents) hair spray, deodorants, perfumes, colognes Ammonia Charcoal briquettes Cleaning fluids Compound 3-weed killers Denatured alcohol

	Enamel
	Gasoline
	Hand signal flares
	Kerosene
	Lacquer
	Leather dressing or bleach
	Lighter fluids (pocket, charcoal camp stove, lamp or torch)
	Liquors
	Matches
	Oil stains for wood
	Paint, flammable
	Paint/varnish remover
	Petroleum products (kerosene, gas, oil)
Flammables (cont.):	Photographic flash bulbs/lamps
	Polishes, liquid (metal, stove, wood furniture)
	Propane tanks (non-purged)
	Propane or other gas used for cooking/heating purposes
	Shellac
	Shoe polish (liquid)
	Solvents (plastic)
	Stains
	Turpentine
	Varnish
	Windshield Solvent
	Wines
	Wood Filler
Gases, Compressed:	Engine, starting fluids
	Fire extinguishers
	Gases used in welding
	Scuba diving tanks (see Note 2)

Rags soaked in Flammables or corrosive substances

Note I: Denotes items which are not completely prohibited from shipment, but rather that shipment by a household goods or unaccompanied baggage carrier is prohibited.

Note 2: Scuba diving tanks may be shipped as household goods or UB provided they have been purged (completely empty).

SHOULD THIS ITEM BE PACKED?

CHAPTER SEVEN

SHOULD THIS ITEM BE PACKED?

Now and then, at the beginning of a move, a customer will approach me, clutching an item that might run halfway between breakable and not...items like a bowling ball, a wood statue, a brass elephant, a basketball, or a carved coconut, to name a few. More often than not, in an effort to make life a little easier for the customer, I let he or she off the hook with many of these items. "Naw", I would say. "I'll take care of it."

I would treat these items as space fillers. I'd wrap them, tuck them between the legs of chairs, or slip them into whatever empty space I could find. After a while, I had to consider whether or not I was expending too much of my own labor in seeing that all these items were secured. I finally figured out that I was, in fact, wasting precious time and effort and using lots of pads.

Had these items been packed in cartons, life for me would have been much simpler. My reasons are as follows:

#1- Particularly in your situation, one carton will cost you much less than several rented pads.
#2 -Packed items are better protected than padded items.
#3 -A simple fondness for the easy way...I'd much rather dolly a load than carry one.

With regard to your goods, if there's ever any question, my answer is now and ever shall be..."pack it!"

HOW TO FOLD AND TAPE A CARTON

CHAPTER EIGHT

HOW TO FOLD AND TAPE A CARTON

As you read this heading you probably thought to yourself, "Everyone knows how to fold and tape a carton. What can this guy tell us?"

First of all, I can tell you that NOT everyone knows how to fold and tape a carton. I have seen folks fold the bottom flaps of a carton in the interlock position and, without using any tape, fill the carton until it weighed upwards of eighty pounds or more. This technique has created many disasters. Below are some illustrations.

Illustration #1- The wrong method. The carton will be uneven. The bottom of the carton will be weaker.

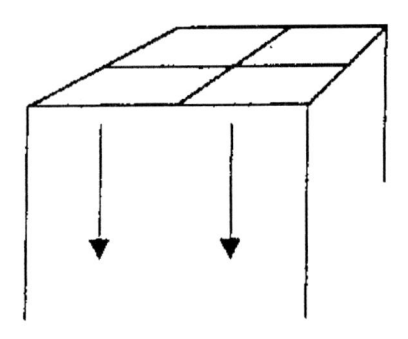

Illustration #2 - The correct method of folding flaps. The dotted line designates the taping method.

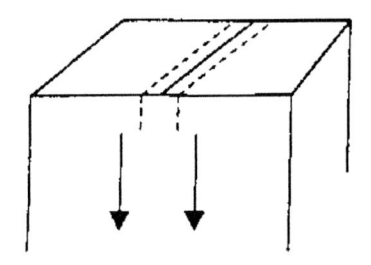

For top and bottom
of carton

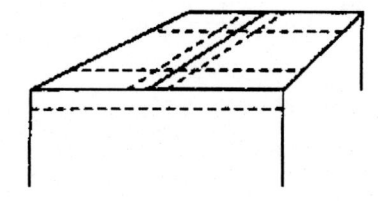

Illustration #3 - This method is for cartons that will spend some time in storage. This method prevents tiny bugs and spiders from invading the contents.

OVERALL RECOMMENDATIONS

CHAPTER NINE

OVERALL RECOMMENDATIONS

As we get into the intricacies of packing, I've listed several recommendations relative to every carton you'll ever fill, regardless of contents.

#1 Be sure to tape the bottom of each carton well enough so that there's no danger of it giving way.

#2 Always fill each carton to the top, but only high enough to allow you to fold the flaps, close the carton, and tape the top.

#3 Mark the contents of each carton you pack. This will tell you it's approximate destination in your new residence, and whether or not it demands critical attention. Marking the contents could also prevent rummaging through a vast array of cartons in search of that all important TV remote, cellular phone, a child's favorite toy, or your check book.

#4 Try not to laugh too hard at this one. Be certain the carton is right side up before you start to pack it. Otherwise, it might accidentally travel upside down throughout the entire trip, which could be fatal to the contents.

If you're finding difficulty in determining the top from the bottom, look for the carton's dimensions, measurements, or trademarks. These are normally found on the bottom of every carton.

#5 Pack nothing hot, like a freshly used steam iron, or dripping wet dishes or damp bath towels. Any of these can cause you multiple problems.

PACKING FURNITURE

CHAPTER TEN

PACKING FURNITURE

If you're so inclined, then by all means, load up those dresser drawers. However, a word of caution...don't pack them too heavy. Remember, you're the one responsible for moving it to and from the truck.

Before you attempt to jam those drawers, check the strength of the legs, the dresser backing, and drawer bottoms. Be sure to avoid packing them so full that they become stuck or hard to open or close. Overfilling could warp or break the sliders, and cost you a small fortune in repairs.

I ask you....is anything more irritating than trying to retrieve a pair of clean underwear from a dresser with a stuck drawer?

I would also advise against packing cologne bottles and knick knacks in dresser drawers. The odds are seven in ten that something will spill or break.

Paper wrap those tiny pieces of jewelry, photos, papers, and similar objects. Small or flat items have been known to sneak over the side of a drawer, drop down the back, and successfully escape through the bottom of many a dresser.

I've never been an advocate of filling furniture drawers, particularly if I couldn't guarantee that the piece of furniture would not be carried upright to the truck, or loaded in the same manner as it would normally sit in the home. You'll probably have occasion to load such items as night stands, small chests, cabinets, and lamp tables on their backs or sides in the truck. You'll be less hindered if you don't have to concern yourself with how the contents of the drawers will react. Before succumbing to the temptation to fill every space and cranny in a drawer, give some thought to how costly it can be.

If you find you're running low on space or cartons, by all means, fill those empty suitcases, travel bags, and hampers.... Yes, hampers! Wicker and basket hampers travel better when they're full, and accommodate bedding, linens, and towels very nicely.

Other furniture pieces that can carry a load are highboy chests, cedar chests, footlockers, and trunks.

For garage items such as small tools, bike parts, skates, and stray pieces, I've found large trash cans to be quite suitable.

PACK LAST

CHAPTER ELEVEN

PACK LAST

I realize that placing the 'pack last' segment of this booklet ahead of the 'pack first' segment may seem to you to be putting the cart before the horse. However, you'll have to trust me. I have good reason. I guess had I changed the title to 'save for last', it would have made more sense..."Oh well!"

The advice I'm about to give you is based on the assumption that you have one or two days before you have to muscle the goods on the truck. The items I'm about to list are only a suggestion of the basics. What and how much you'll actually need will hinge on the size of the move, and the time it will take to complete it.

Try to save only the bare necessities for last...a few dishes and pieces of silverware, toiletries, medical items, a couple of towels, and a change or two of clothing. For me, the bare essentials consist of soap, a towel, one change of clothing, and the coffee pot, complete with cup.

I'm forced to admit that without that hot, fresh coffee to start my day, I could not even read this publication, let alone follow it's direction.

It wouldn't hurt to keep the tool box handy for dismantling and disassembling whatever furniture is necessary for transport. Also, if you're so inclined, save the vacuum cleaner, cleaning supplies, a broom and mop, some trash bags, and rags.

Try to avoid saving too many items for last. The idea is to spend as little time as possible in final preparation come moving day.

MY WAY

CHAPTER TWELVE

MY WAY

Throughout the packing segment of this publication, I'll be directing you as you wrap various items to place the item in a diagonal position, either on newsprint or on a paper pad. Please keep in mind that this method is only my preference, and not necessarily the law of the land.

For me, it's quicker and easier to handle four corners than four sides. I use the same method in wrapping small and flat pieces of furniture when loading. I guess after twenty plus years, it's become more a matter of habit than anything else. Although, I do feel that the package looks more professional with the diagonal method.

There must be something to my madness. The next time you buy a hot dog or a sub sandwich take a look at how it was wrapped. Take a moment, try wrapping any item you choose squarely, then diagonally, and time yourself. You might find the results interesting.

PACK FIRST

CHAPTER THIRTEEN

PACK FIRST

This section of the publication will take you through the most intricate and tedious phase of the move, and probably the most important in terms of damage control and out- of- pocket cost.

From this moment on, chances are you'll be too busy to sit around watching videos, reading books, or listening to cassettes or discs. Even at your destination, your plans for any of the above could be thwarted for some time, depending on how big a job lay ahead. So....why not start packing the non-critical items.

Entertainment

Now that you're into the 'busy mode', let's begin by packing the entertainment items... books, records, videos, albums, discs, and stereo components.

Books

Books, particularly hard cover books, should be packed tightly on end with bindings facing up. You can use paperbacks, soft cover books, magazines and periodicals to fill bottom spaces and to lay flat across the top to fill the carton. Magazines like National Geographic can be packed the same way as hard cover books to prevent corners of pages being turned or damaged.

I've never found the need to paper wrap books, either individually or in small bundles, except for special editions, expensive leather bound collector's items, or manuscripts. The monetary value you yourself place on these books should determine the method you choose.

Either way, one of your primary concerns should be to pack the carton as tightly as possible to inhibit movement. This rule should apply to every carton you pack, regardless of content. Books should also be packed in small cartons.

Records and Albums

Records and albums in jackets should be packed in small cartons on end. Paper wrap all unjacketed albums singly and place them on end. Also, again... the tighter, the better.

Videos

Videos in jackets should be stacked side by side like albums, also in small cartons. Again, if they're not jacketed, pack them singly and stack on end. Do not lay them flat, as any amount of weight placed on top of them could crack the plastic casing.

Cassettes

I would suggest paper wrapping three or four to a bundle. This also applies to stereo cartridges. I'd use a small carton for these. If you happen to have a carrying case, simply leave them in the case. Paper wrap the entire case, cassettes and all, and place the entire package in a larger carton. Everything should be perfectly safe.

Discs

Pack them in a small carton exactly like albums. I have heard reports of discs being ruined in shipping. However, in researching, I have confirmed that damage occurred only when the discs passed through airport X-ray machines. To my knowledge, no danger exists relating to adverse hot or cold weather in shipping.

Air shipping disks

If by chance, you are making plans to air ship a carton or two of disks, contingencies do exist. Many electronic stores furnish aluminum jackets designed to protect the disk through X-ray detection.

Stereos and Components

If you didn't save the original cartons for all these items, then I strongly advise you to turn to the dish pack. Choose the heaviest and largest component first, wrap it tightly in a paper pad, and set it flatly on the bottom. Then choose the next heaviest component, wrap it in a paper pad, and set it directly on top of the previous item. Repeat the same procedure until the dish pack is full or until all the components are packed. Normally, a dish pack can hold up to five items.

Always pack the turntable on the top. Use plenty of crumpled newsprint along the sides of each item to prevent movement, and a good thick layer between each item for added protection. If the turntable has no plastic lid, crumple up a few extra sheets and cushion the top.

Speakers

If you don't have original speaker cartons, wrap them diagonally in a paper pad. Wrapping them could pay off a hundredfold. If necessary, they could be transported without any further wrapping, providing you use extreme caution as to where and how they are to be loaded in the truck.

Wiring

As with most stereo components, there are seemingly miles of speaker wires and connecting lines. Disconnecting and reconnecting stereo systems is not one of my strongest suites. For me, the simplest method has always been to disconnect only enough wires and cables to separate each component.

I usually roll and rubber band the loose wiring and wrap it with the component. I've never been required to reconnect any stereos at destination, so I'm not at liberty to advise, except to read the technical directions that accompany the product, or develop a great memory in a big hurry.

Pictures-Mirrors

I'm referring to the large pictures, paintings, and mirrors that are mounted on the wall, as well as those mirrors that are attached to a dresser or vanity. Here is where the paper pad and section type picture carton will serve you best.

Let's begin by laying a paper pad flat on the floor and placing your picture or painting face down in the center, and diagonally across the pad. Fold and tape all the ends, lean it on its end against a flat surface, out of harms way, and follow the same procedure with the next item. Wrap them all and consolidate them in one location.

If you should run across a picture or painting too large for one pad to cover, simply lay two paper pads side by side with one overlapping the other just slightly. Tape the two paper pads together, and you now have one very large paper pad.

Now that you've completed the paper wrap segment, start forming and taping the sections of each carton. You should see on one end of each section two long flaps and one four inch flap in me middle. Fold the short flap first and then both long flaps, one over the other.

Next, sort through the items you've wrapped and try to separate the various sizes into matching groups. If for some reason, none of your items match inside, don't be concerned. In many instances, you may be able to slip two or three items into one carton depending on the thickness of each item, which is one reason I directed you to group them. If any of your packages contain a painting with a gingerbread type jutting frame, I strongly advise you to pack that alone.

Assuming you need four sections to cover two medium size pictures, make them up and connect the two bottom corners around the packages. If the two sections overlap, you're on the right track. Next, connect the two top sections together as you did the bottoms. Besides overlapping each other, they should overlap the two bottom sections as well. If they do, your packages should be completely covered. Tape them all together or tie them with strong twine, mark the contents, add a couple of arrows to distinguish the top from the bottom, and you've completed your first picture carton. Here's an illustration, just in case!

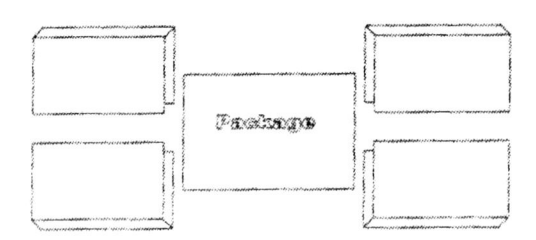

This is usually a good spot for any poster. If you're in doubt about packing more than one item per carton, by all means, pack only one. There's no need to squeeze if there's the slightest possibility of damage.

Not all items will require four sections. Some may require only two, and in some cases, I've gotten away with one.

On the other hand, if a painting is too large for four sections, then perhaps six or eight will do. This is known as the telescope method, or customizing if you like. Begin as you did with four sections, hooking them into the four corners of the painting. Then add whatever sections you need to completely cover the painting. Once the entire painting is covered, tape or tie them altogether. Be sure to run the twine the length and width of the item to secure all loose sections.
Following is an illustration to help you.

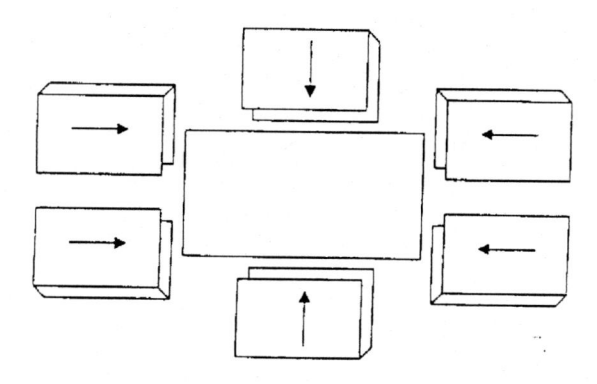

When tying this telescoped carton, my preference is to follow the dotted lines in the illustration below.

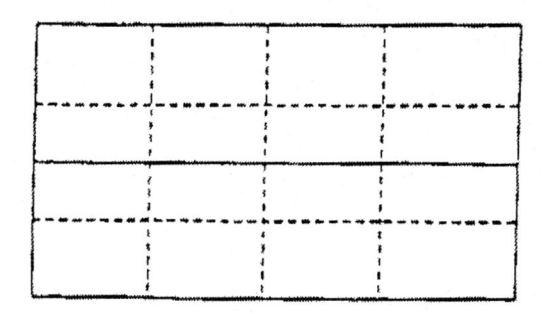

37

The following is an illustration using only two sections

Flat Glass

Packing glass shelves or unframed mirrors is not as intimidating as it seems. Long, thin, flat, fragile, unprotected glass is as simple to pack as any picture or painting.

Begin by wrapping two or more glass shelves, up to four of equal size, diagonally centered in one paper pad. Separate each piece by only one sheet of unprinted news. Wrap them tightly and make sure the ends are even. If you have enough glass for two or more packages... great!

Next, fit two sections of picture carton around each end. Cut the sections down to within four inches of the top of the packages. Fold the ends and sides over the packages and tape or tie. Mark the contents, add the words 'fragile-glass', and the shelves are done. Where one shelf is fragile, three or four are very strong. There's safety in numbers.

The only answer for that wall mirror or that single sheet of glass, is a wood crate...normally! If crating is really out of the question financially, then I'll explain how I would handle it. First, I'd wrap it twice in paper pads, and if it bowed even slightly, I'd wrap it a third time. Then, using picture carton sections, instead of folding and taping them, I'd wrap them singly around the package making sure the ends were well protected. It's survival will ultimately depend on how carefully it's handled and where exactly it's placed on the truck.

Marble-glass table tops

Marble is another tricky item, and should definitely be crated. However, if packed exactly like you packed the single sheet of glass, chances are it too will reach it's destination intact...providing it's only a small piece, and not too heavy.

Heavy large marble pieces and thick glass table tops are absolutely 'must be crated' items. Chances are good that a third party service can solve your problem.

Bulletin Boards

There's really no need to remove the legion of notes tacked to the bulletin board. Simply lay it flat on it's back, wrap it as is in a paper pad, exactly as you would a picture or painting. The paper pad should keep the contents intact. The worst that could possibly happen, is a little ruffled artwork.

KITCHEN ITEMS

CHAPTER FOURTEEN

KITCHEN ITEMS

Can goods

The average can of soup or beans doesn't weigh much more than fifteen or sixteen ounces. However, a small carton with fifty or sixty cans could weigh almost as much as a carton of books. Small cartons are the magic words here. Stack each can upright, one on top of the other. Top the carton off with bag foods or kitchen linens. Tape the top and mark the contents. That was easy!

Bottles-jar foods

Pack the heaviest bottles and jars on the bottom. Use a small carton, as a bunch of these can also get heavy. Using a couple of sheets of unprinted news per bottle or jar, wrap each one loosely and place upright in the carton. Be sure to tape the caps or lids of all the bottles or jars that have been previously opened to prevent leakage. If necessary, you can top off the carton with wrapped bundles of cooking utensils or kitchen linens.

After taping the carton, mark the contents 'fragile' and 'keep upright'. This is one carton that must not be loaded anyway but right side up.

Box foods-spices

I usually pack all box foods, cereals, and the like upright. I've never found the need to wrap these items, except that I always tape open boxes to keep from spilling all the corn flakes.

Small spice cans can be wrapped in bundles of three or four, and spice jars in twos. I've never had to be concerned about laying spice jars on their sides. They seem quite solid. As a matter of fact, they make a very good top filler for dish packs or medium cartons.

Cleaning items (under the sink)

I would basically follow the same procedure as 'box foods'. Tape the caps of previously opened bottles, make sure caps and lids are tight, tape open boxes shut. Keep all bottles and jars upright including, and especially, spray bottles. Mark the proper contents, add arrows or write 'do not tip' all around the carton.

Small appliances

Toasters, blenders, can openers, food processors, mixers, toaster-ovens, waffle irons, etc. can be packed in a large carton' providing they are wrapped properly (triplicate is nice) and cushioned well. Some folks prefer the strong, unyielding dish pack, but then there's that old budget to think about. Be sure to disassemble mixers before you pack them.

Pots and pans

These are definitely among the simplest of kitchen items to pack. Medium and large cartons are perfectly suited to handle these objects. The same goes for almost all non-breakable cooking items, including Tupperware and plastics. I never used more than one sheet of paper to pack this type of item. The only trick here will be to conserve space. Once in a while, I'll use the large kettles and deep pots for the real small kitchen items, but only if I'm short of cartons. It can be rather time consuming.

Silverware-junk drawer-sharp knives

If your silverware is nesting in plastic trays, why not wrap the entire tray, silverware and all. The same can go for the so-called 'junk drawer' items or nail and screw bins. My idea of packing a junk drawer is to line a small waste- paper basket with paper, pull the drawer, and dump the contents. I then wrap the top of the basket to prevent spillage, and drop the whole thing into a medium or large carton.

Sharp knives, meat forks, and pins can be a hazard to your health if you're not extremely careful. I try to find a large Tupperware tray or something solid to place them in. If I fail at that, then I'll pack them altogether, very loosely, in several sheets of paper, then mark the package accordingly for safety at destination when unpacking.

Dishes

Since you'll be too busy to cook for company, let's pack the formal dishes first, including the wine glasses, the stemware, and silver set. You'll need a dish pack, lots of unprinted news, and if a silver set is to be included, some tissue paper.

Many sets of fine china include such luxuries as zippered pouches. These pouches usually hold an entire set of dinner plates. You probably have pouches for the salad plates, the saucers, and other dishes as well. If you're really fortunate, each of these plates is separated by a protective felt pad, or some type of doily. Assuming you do, and all the pads are in place, the first step is to wrap the entire pouch in one package. We'll begin with the dinner plates, usually the heaviest items, for the bottom of the dish pack.

To best explain how to wrap it, I'll ask you to lay out a stack of unprinted news and position yourself at one corner. Set the pouch in the center of the paper, and using only the top sheet of paper, fold the corner nearest you over the pouch. As you hold the first corner over the pouch, fold the left corner of the paper over that. Hold that down, then fold the right corner. Finally, flip the entire pouch toward the farthest corner.

Now, with the first sheet of paper completely enveloping the pouch, flip the entire package upside down, place it in the center of the paper and repeat the entire procedure with the second sheet. If the need suits you, repeat with a third sheet. To make sure this rather large package stays wrapped, you may want to seal it with a piece of tape. Once that's done, place the package in the bottom corner of the dish pack .on end.

You can repeat that same procedure with salad plates, saucers, soup dishes, and platters. For that matter, with every item that occupies a pouch.

If you don't enjoy the luxury of a pouch, then we'll make our own. Grab four plates and set them next to the paper stack Ready? Lay one plate in the center of the paper stack. Position yourself, fold one sheet of paper from the corner nearest you over the plate. Next, lay the second plate over the paper, but directly on top of the first plate. Fold a sheet over the second plate and repeat the same procedure or the next two plates. You now have your home-made pads or doilies. It's time to make the pouch. Fold the left corner sheets over the package and then the right. Now, flip the package upside down toward the far corner, then slide the package back toward the center of the paper stack. Follow the whole procedure, this time using two sheets of paper. You now have four plates in a pouch with four pads, using only six sheets of paper.

I will caution you once again to stand all plates on end in the carton. I would not advise packing too many plates to a package. You'll reach a point where the paper won't cover as much as it should and the paper will also lose it's cushioning affect.

Let's move on to the not so flat items...cups. Cups require only a slight variation. You're back in position (one corner of the paper stack). Lay the cup on it's side, handle facing you. Flip one sheet of paper, the corner nearest you, over the cup, roll the cup a half turn, bring the left and right corners of the paper loosely over the cup, then roll the cup to the far corner, wrapping as you go. Wrapped in a single sheet of paper, the cup should be well cushioned and the package should now be two to three times the actual size of the cup.

Now that you've packed all the flatware on the bottom and scrunched a layer of paper on top for cushion, you can line the cups (on end) across the carton.

Sugar bowls, creamers, salt and pepper shakers, and stubby glasses should all be as easy as the cups. The same procedure could apply to soup tureens, pitchers, small vases, and knick-knacks.

Once you've successfully packed a few cups, you have obtained the basic knowledge of how to pack most of your breakables. You can determine how many sheets of paper you'll need for various items by how much cushion you judge necessary between items, or how bulky the item is. For instance...stemware will require more paper and cushioning than a coffee cup. Where you used only one sheet for the cup, you may use three on the stemware.

Remember, both the cup and the stemware are much stronger on end than on their sides. Also, the coffee cup, being heavier than the stemware piece, would be packed below the stemware in the carton.

Silver

If there are no protective pouches covering your silver, you must carefully wrap each item in tissue paper before wrapping it in unprinted news to prevent tarnishing. Silver must be treated like glass when packed, with plenty of cushion between pieces.

LAMPS

CHAPTER FIFTEEN

LAMPS

Most lamps, with the exception of the small bedside lights, require the protection of a paper pad and either a customized lamp carton or a dish pack. Remove the shade, the harp, and the light bulb. Roll the cord around the base or neck of the lamp and place it diagonally across the center of a paper pad.

Imagine, if you will, that you're about to wrap a huge coffee cup or glass. The procedure and result should be exactly the same. Tape the loose end of the paper pad and place it right side up in the carton. Framed family photos, wrapped and tucked along the inside walls of the carton, make good fillers, as do the harps. Don't be afraid to pack light bulbs, knick-knacks and other breakables with the lamps, as long as they are well wrapped and cushioned.

Shades

There are many common sense ways to pack more than one lamp shade in a single carton. The trick is to keep them separated and well protected. The magic word here is paper. Not just scrunched paper, but carefully placed paper.

Gather up all the shades in one spot. Grab an extra large carton, lay one or two sheets across the inside bottom of the carton and you're ready.

First, we'll work on the assumption that you have several shades that vary in size, but are shaped the same. Place the smallest shade in the bottom center of the carton, right side up. Gently lay one or two sheets of paper over the top. Place the second slightly larger shade over the first one, and paper over that. If you still have room, do the same with the third shade and paper over it.

If the carton is almost full, don't try to squeeze another shade in. Lay paper gently over the top and scrunch just enough sheets loosely around the sides and corners to prevent movement. Be sure to mark the contents and the word 'fragile' all around the carton.

Dry run-lamp shades

Let's work on those shades that neither match in size or shape. Make up your carton, as before, with a layer of paper across the bottom. Next, let's experiment with a couple of shades without the paper. For example, place the first shade right side up, and the second on it's side. Keep in mind that the shades will be separated and protected with paper, and that neither must touch the other. Be careful that they don't overlap the carton top and prevent closure.

If the dry run is successful, you've solved your problem. If not, use smaller cartons and pack them separately. The idea behind the dry run is to try to consolidate space and limit the number of cartons necessary.

Floral arrangements

These can either be very simple to pack or very difficult and time consuming. There seems to be no in between. If yours happens to be one of the simple ones, then pretend it's a lamp shade. Find a suitable carton and follow tbe same 'gentle' procedure. Unlike lamp shades, floral arrangements are a one to a carton item.

If your entry way happens to be lined with artificial trees, or your floral arrangement runs the length of your dining room, please read the next chapter and study the illustrations very carefully.

CAPPING

CHAPTER SIXTEEN

CAPPING

You've packed all the lamps in the house.. all but one! You're staring at a thirty six inch clear glass behemoth that's standing on a small lamp table near the window. You didn't purchase any special lamp cartons. It never occurred to you. Suddenly, your son rambles out of his room and presents you with three trophies. As you turn to face your son, your eyes lock onto your wife's favorite piece of driftwood above the fireplace mantle. You panic.

You have barely enough wardrobes for the clothes...so much for the tall cartons! You turn to the dish pack. You sigh, It's only twenty seven inches deep. Ten inches too short. Not to worry!

You recall back in the picture packing section how you successfully telescope-packed a very large painting. Now, you are about to telescope or cap a very tall lamp, three trophies, and a piece of driftwood.

Once you have the items wrapped and ready (no need to wrap the driftwood), place them in a dish pack with whatever other fillers may be lying around. Tape the top flaps of the dish pack together in the upright position. The carton has just become nine inches taller. Add more fillers if you like.

If you still need more depth, no problem. Let's assume you need another five inches. Grab a medium carton. Leaving both ends open, slip the flaps of the medium over the dish pack. Inch it downward until the top of the medium carton is about one to two inches above the tallest item in the dish pack. Add more fillers. Tape the medium carton to the dish pack, cushion the tallest item and close the flaps. Mark the contents and consider the problem solved.

This page contains illustrations. Imagine the plant as your lamp and trophies.

After placing the item inside the bottom carton, slip the flaps of the top carton over the bottom flaps and inch the top carton downward to approximately two inches from the top of the object. Tape both cartons together and mark it well. This package must be kept upright at all times.

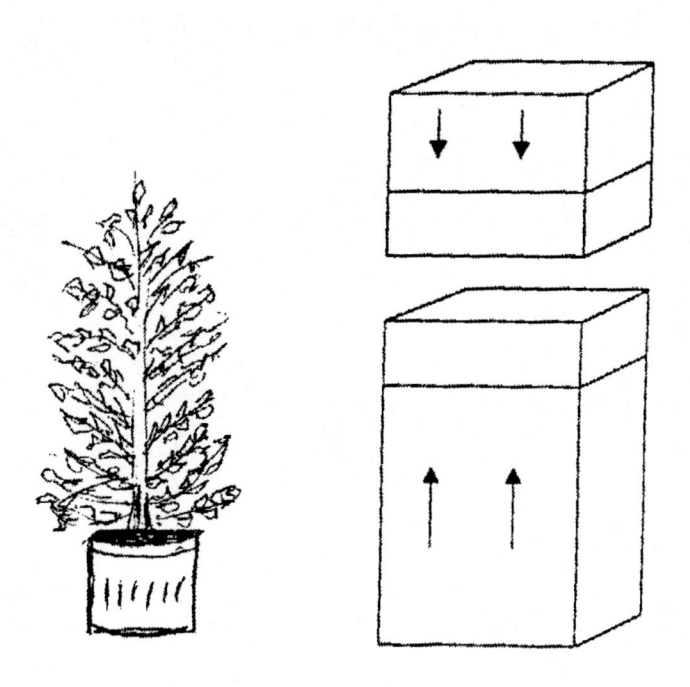

Keeping the floral arrangement upright, slide the two cartons together sideways. Tape and mark accordingly.

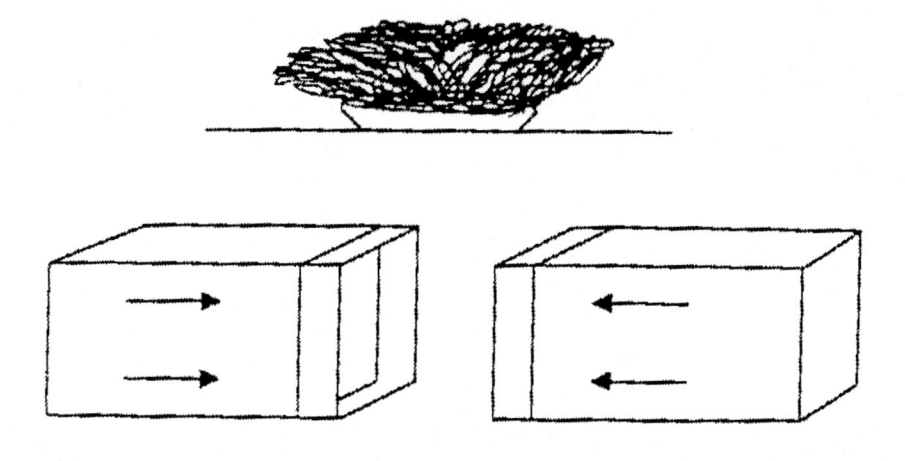

Remember, with a little ingenuity, a good cutting tool, and a roll of tape, you can make a carton almost any size you desire. I have a young son for whom I constructed an imaginary star-wars spacecraft out of several used wardrobes and a roll of tape. The craft still exists today after several months, and measures 10'x10'x6'.

He's played in it, slept in it, stocked it with space travel stuff, and even had a few friends over. This might give you dads and granddads some ideas about what to do with the cartons after the move.

COMPUTERS

CHAPTER SEVENTEEN

COMPUTERS

You could hardly call this author a computer buff. My knowledge of computer operation is absolutely nil. However, I am quite familiar with the packing and transportation of the computer, it's components, and other electronic gadgets. Although, I must confess, I learned one lesson the hard way. When readying a home computer for packing, I smartly disconnected the wall plug, and promptly erased weeks of stored memory. Needless to say, that happened only once. Since you'll be packing your own computer, you needn't worry that I'll show up to disconnect it.

If you saved the original cartons, as most folks do, then you've saved yourself time and money, providing you solve the foam insert riddle. Trust me, I have frequently experienced some terrible frustration trying to fix those foam inserts into their original positions.

Once you've disconnected the components, be sure to remove the paper trays and loose catch baskets. Then, wrap each one in a paper pad as you did your stereo components. Remember the aforementioned 'bubble pack', if that's your preference. If you don't have the original cartons, then choose a carton that will not only hold the component, but provide at least an inch of space on all sides. I would not advise placing any component on it's side, except for the keyboard. I could also not advise trying to consolidate all the components into one large carton as the weight could be considerable...and dangerous.

Monitors, keyboards, and speakers usually fit well inside a dish pack, as do some printers and processors. However, if any component is too large, place it in a larger carton, then cut the carton down or customize it for that particular item. Remember to scrunch enough sheets of paper around and on top of the object to keep it tightly packed and protected. All that's left is to seal and properly mark the carton.

Other pieces of electronics should be treated in the same manner... typewriters, calculators, fax machines, copiers, shredders, etc.

If you own a copier, you may already be aware of the service required involving 'ink' in some of the older models.

LINENS

CHAPTER EIGHTEEN

LINENS

You may have already used most of your linens as fillers for other cartons. If not, these are easy items to dispose of. Simply lay one or two sheets of paper across the bottom of a medium or large carton. Pack the folded linen as is to the top of the carton. Spread a couple of sheets over the top and you're done.

It's not unusual to find all sorts of goodies in the linen closet. I've found candles, bags of ribbon, Christmas wrap, and a wide range of collectibles. It seems feasible to pack them with the linens, since that's where they will probably all end up at destination. However, separate anything that might spill or be prepared for a lot of grief.

Since we're doing linens, a word of caution regarding the use of sheets and towels to wrap breakables...Don't! Neither sheets nor towels have any cushioning effect on fragile items, whatsoever. Dust prevention is the most you can hope for. It's one mistake many people make all too frequently.

BATHROOM ITEMS

CHAPTER NINETEEN

BATHROOM ITEMS

If your bathroom is anything like mine, it will contain everything from wall pictures, medicines, cosmetics, toiletries, linens, soap, a waste basket, scales, a box of tissue, and of course yesterday's sports page. Instead of separating everything into groups, I prefer to consolidate the entire inventory into one or two cartons, if possible. Common sense and paper can eliminate any problem here.

Pack the heaviest objects on the bottom, the scale on it's side, and pictures standing against the side walls of the carton. Before you go any further, line the inside of your empty waste basket with paper and fill it to the top with your smallest objects like lipsticks, combs, brushes, medicine bottles, small packs of this and that, and place the basket upright inside the carton. The rest is repetition. Remember, this carton must be loaded upright on the truck.

There's something about packing bathroom items that always bothers me. It's not so much packing the stuff, as knowing that sooner or later, I'll have to unpack it, sort it all out, and put it all away.

CLOSET ITEMS

CHAPTER TWENTY

CLOSET ITEMS

Packing a wardrobe is simply moving an item of clothing from one wardrobe bar to another. Not much to think about really! However, there are four necessary steps to be carried out if you expect to prevent a costly cleaning bill.

#1 Pack the clothes tightly enough to prevent any hanger movement.
#2 Be certain the hangers are strong enough to hold the clothing in transit.
#3 Avoid packing anything in the bottom of a wardrobe.
#4 Remember that the ends of the bar are resting on cardboard, so do not load the wardrobe too heavily.

Shoes-purses

If your shoes are in boxes, you have no problem. A medium or large carton will do just fine. If your shoes aren't in boxes, you still have no problem. Grab the nearest pair of shoes, turn one upside down, then turn it opposite the other shoe so that the toe of one is against the opening of the other. This helps to prevent toe scuffing and makes wrapping a little easier.

If your inventory is like mine, you really have no problem. I wrap the one pair of boots, and drop the four pairs of tennis shoes like potatoes in a bin.

I always wrap purses one at a time. Some get scuffed or rubbed easily. Instead of guessing which ones do and don't, I wrap 'em all.

Hats

If the lady of the house has a flair for hats, follow the same procedure as the 'dry run' lamp shades...lots of paper.

Neckties

I must admit that I had to do a little experimenting before claiming any kind of success in packing neckties. I tried draping them over wardrobe bars, but some always fell to the bottom and when I slid them inside dresser drawers, some got crumpled. How to pack these items successfully was anybody's' guess for a while. Finally, we've found a method that works like a charm.

Cut a piece of cardboard about eight inches wide and an inch or so longer than your longest tie. Stack your ties, one on top of the other, like you were laying them on a table. Fold a sheet of paper in half and lay it over the ties. Tape over the sheet around the back of the cardboard piece. Next, wrap the whole thing in a half paper pad. This works well.

Belts

I either roll belts for packing or string them on a metal hanger for a wardrobe. Why not leave them in a dresser drawer or pack them with shoes or purses.

Plastic bins and metal racks

These items and shoe racks don't usually require any packing. They are used as space fillers in the truck.

JEWELRY

CHAPTER TWENTY ONE

JEWELRY

Small jewelry boxes and cases are usually packed with bedroom knick-knacks. If the lady of the house happens to have one of those swinging door jewelry cabinets, why not shrink wrap it with the contents intact. Shrink wrapping will protect the contents and the cabinet.

If you're packing your goods for transport by a moving company, empty and pack the contents and shrink wrap the cabinet.

Jewelry packing puts me in mind of a particular move, completed some years ago. Someone's mother who's husband had recently passed away was relocating from California to Tennessee to be near her daughter.

She had done a great job packing her cartons. However, to make a long story short, as we unloaded her items at her destination, she kept demanding to see the top of every carton my crew and I set down. No one gave it any thought until the job was completed.

As she was signing the paperwork, she remarked, "I see you boys didn't take anything this time. I said, "Pardon me?!" She immediately led me to a carton and showed me the little scheme she had devised to detect any theft. "They got to me the last time we moved", she said.

She had made a single pencil mark across the top of each carton from one flap to the other, crossing the tape line. The mark was barely visible. Had anyone removed the original tape and tried to reseal the carton, she would have known. Food for thought!

Coins

Any open container full of coins poses a problem. It's not a good idea to leave coins rattling around. Stuff the container with old rags or a towel and pack it out of sight.

Wedding gifts

You newlyweds with scores of wedding gifts stacked around your apartment.. ..congratulations! I realize most of your gifts are still in their original cartons. However, most of these cartons offer no more protection than from dust. Why not consolidate all those small cartons into large cartons. This will increase their protection and save truck space. Before you pack, be sure to return the second and third toasters. No need to work any harder than necessary.

TOYS

CHAPTER TWENTY TWO

TOYS

This little word can involve a world of items deserving of a publication all its own. I'll start with the basic small toys and try to include the larger complicated ones along the way.

First of all, do not pack any stuffed animals. They are excellent for cushioning the breakable toys and for filling empty spaces in any carton. Incidentally, before you pack any battery operated toy, remove the batteries. Batteries can leak and ruin a toy, or the toy could be accidentally turned on while in the carton, if jostled, and run down during transport.

Again, when packing toys, you're in an area where more than a normal amount of paper is usually required. That is why I recommended not packing the stuffed animals. I'm not above loading up a toy chest for transport to save space, providing I can secure the lid and not hear any rattling noises. Rattling is a danger sign in any carton.

Most small toys usually take a large carton. I would use an extra large carton only when packing very light items or an oversized toy. Tricycles, bikes, scooters, and doll carriages don't normally require cartons. However, I do wrap many of these items as I have large dolls and large model planes and trucks. It's a judgement call on your part as to how safely the item will travel in transport, or how expensive or critical the item is.

Games

Table games may have to be packed on end to fit into a large carton. If so, scotch tape the lid of each game carton on all four sides to prevent spillage and loss, not so much for the monetary value, as for the aggravation of having to pick up the many tiny pieces.

Easels, chalkboards, and small game tables should be wrapped in paper pads. Be sure to mark the contents. Small portable televisions, radios, clocks, and computer games should be paper padded and packed in a dish pack. If a full paper pad is too large, cut it in half or thirds. Sections are easier to handle for small items and could save much wasted space.

If by chance you are planning to move a sand box (sand and all), pack the sand in buckets, not cartons. Many years ago I attempted to move a carton of sand, my customer had so carefully packed. Needless to say, the bottom fell out. To this day, every time I sweep the trailer floor, I discover some of that sand.

Doll houses

Doll houses should be emptied of all furnishings and cleared of all loose or moving items. Houses are usually pad wrapped in the truck for transport. However, if this house is unusual and you feel it requires packing, measure the dimensions and follow the capping or telescoping procedure.

Many people are not aware that in some European countries, particularly in the event of an international move, every single item in the home is packed in cartons, whether it be the smallest knick-knack or the largest piece of furniture, including appliances and upholstery. Cartons are built on the job to fit whatever piece is required. The cost of labor and materials must be phenomenal.

FIXTURES

CHAPTER TWENTY THREE

FIXTURES

Drapes- blinds

Drapes, like kitchen stoves, were once very common items in a moving van. The last few years have seen both items go the way of the built-ins. However, if drapes are included in your inventory, one of the simplest methods is to fold them at the pleats and hang them from a hanger in a wardrobe, or drape them directly over the wardrobe bar. Either way, they'll have to be secured to prevent them falling to the bottom. If they're draped over the bar, wrap a string or twine around both hanging ends just under the bar. If they're on a hanger, do the same just under the hanger bar and tie the hanger to the bar. Be careful that the drapes never touch the bottom of the wardrobe.

Blinds should be raised tightly to the rod and the drawstring rolled up and secured. I wrap all blinds separately in a paper pad. Traverse rods, curtain and drapery rods, should be paper padded also, or at least bundled and taped.

Chandeliers

Here's another item that screams for a wood crate. However, let me relate to you an ingenious alternative I discovered a few years ago from a retired Navy man. His chandelier, loaded with dangling crystals, measured three and a half feet in length and almost that in diameter.

He cut down a used refrigerator carton he had salvaged from an appliance store, sawed off the ends of an old broom, and shoved it through small holes at each end of the carton near the top from which to hang the item.

He hung the chandelier from the broom handle and secured it with twine to prevent it from falling, then tied each end of the chandelier to the sides of the carton to prevent movement of any kind. Next he spread a blanket and scrunched paper across the bottom of the carton to cushion the chandelier in the event it fell. Only four tiny crystals came loose in the course of the move, but were found unscathed in the bottom of the carton.

Ceiling fan

It's a matter of removing the blades, wrapping the element in a paper pad, and packing the works in a large carton. If yours has lights, remove the blades, bulbs, globes, and pack away. Unlike a chandelier, it's not necessary to hang a ceiling fan element.

SEWING MACHINES

CHAPTER TWENTY FOUR

SEWING MACHINES

Although a sewing machine cabinet itself doesn't require packing, it's contents certainly do. By contents, I mean the machine, or 'head' as it's referred to, and those six little drawers loaded with buttons, needles, thread, pins, and every other tiny item connected to the business of sewing.

It's a simple matter to free each drawer, wrap it, contents and all, and pack it inside a carton. It's such a miserable job to pick all the contents up off the floor.

Most heads require only two screws to be turned to release it from the cabinet. Once it's free, a book carton is perfect for this item.

GRANDFATHER CLOCK

CHAPTER TWENTY FIVE

GRANDFATHER CLOCK

Any attempt at moving this item without first securing it's loose hanging inners, could totally destroy it. The items to remove and pack are the two weights, the pendulum, and the key (if applicable). The chains must also be secured to prevent scratching or breaking the glass front. This can be accomplished by rolling it up and tying it off, or by taping it to the backside wall. If you're planning the latter, be careful the tape doesn't harm the finish.

THROW RUGS

CHAPTER TWENTY SIX

THROW RUGS

If you haven't already used them as fillers, gather two or three at a time, roll them up in a bundle, and tie or wrap them in a paper pad.

Larger rugs should be rolled evenly and tied at each end. Expensive rugs should be rolled and wrapped in brown paper or paper pads.

Never roll a rug and pad together. This can stretch and ruin the shape of the rug and pad.

PIANO BENCH AND MUSIC

CHAPTER TWENTY SEVEN

PIANO BENCH AND MUSIC

Maybe you have two choices. Either empty the bench and pack the music, or remove the bench legs, if you can, and wrap the bench, music intact in a paper pad.

WEAPONS

CHAPTER TWENTY EIGHT

WEAPONS

How you pack these items will depend on a number of things. Is your collection large, small, long weapons, or pistols, guns, spears, or bows and arrows?

If you have long weapons in plastic cases, pad wrap them in the truck. If they are in soft, pliable weapon cases, wrap them in paper pads if you like. If you only have one or two long weapons not covered, paper pad each one.

If your collection contains hand guns or pistols, pack them in a carton. If you have a large collection or long weapons, try a capped dish pack.

Remember never to store a loaded weapon in a carton or anywhere in the truck. An accident or heavy jolt could cause the weapon to discharge.

Ammunition

I cannot advise on packing ammunition, nor how to dispose of it. Insurance regulations have always prohibited us from transporting it.

FIREPLACE ITEMS

CHAPTER TWENTY NINE

FIREPLACE ITEMS

I usually wrap the fireplace tools and stand in one bundle in a paper pad. Andirons, grate, screen, and log basket will usually fit somewhere in the van and need no special attention. If you plan to move any firewood, it would be wise to pack it. However, do not pack it too heavy.

LONG ITEMS

CHAPTER THIRTY

LONG ITEMS

Umbrellas, canes, driftwood, closet poles, and shower rods require no more than bundling and tape, or paper pad if you prefer.

MATTRESSES

CHAPTER THIRTY ONE

MATTRESSES

I much prefer to 'shrink wrap' all mattresses and box springs, regardless of size, to packing them in cartons for a number of reasons.

#1 Many of the larger mattresses are heavy and cumbersome. Shrink wrap will give slightly, but will limit sagging and will make handling the mattress much easier.
#2 Cardboard tears too easily. Shrink wrap doesn't.
#3 If by chance the carton gets wet, you've got inside damage. Not so with shrink wrap.
#4 There are new mattresses on the market that are an inch or two thicker than standard, and I for one, have found it difficult finding any suitable cartons to accommodate the thickness.
#5 Shrink wrapping offers much better protection against any possible damage than cardboard cartons.

If you're planning the shrink wrap method, stand your mattress on it's side and shrink wrap lengthwise around the entire mattress. Then, stand it on end and circle the entire width, making certain you've covered the corners.

Use the same procedure for box springs and crib mattresses.

Waterbed mattress

To avoid pinhole leaks or chafing, I have always packed waterbed mattresses in dish packs, capped if necessary. These babies get heavy. Packing eases handling and loading it in the truck.

Futon mattress

There are only two ways I've ever packed one of these.

#1 Roll it and pack it inside a capped wardrobe.
#2 Roll it and shrink wrap it.

Either way, you'll probably be sorry you bought it!

PATIO ITEMS

CHAPTER THIRTY TWO

PATIO ITEM

I'm referring to the glass top...the one that would take all but an act of congress to remove from it's base. I suppose there's a certain amount of luck involved, even with following my advice. If so, then my luck has held well, so far.

The method I always use is to cover the entire table top with a piece of cardboard which I secure with tape. Next, I lay a furniture pad over the top, and finally I shrink wrap over that.

"You're not out of the woods yet!" Loading the table in the right spot on the truck will complete the trick. If your table has a Plexiglas top, a single furniture pad or a paper pad will serve to protect the top from scratching. If you're fortunate enough to easily lift the glass top from your table, paper pad it and add four picture carton sections. Be sure to scrunch lots of paper in those sections for cushion.

Flower Pots

Pottery is much more fragile than it looks and should be packed in dish packs. One mistake people often make is slipping one flower pot inside another when packing. Even with paper, the slightest jostle can split both pots. Cushion them well and keep them separated. You may want to paper pad the large ones.

Concrete

Concrete is heavy and sometimes bulky. Worse yet, it is fragile and easily cracked or chipped. It's weight demands a strong carton. It's another item that may need extra paper pads and lots of cushion. A dish pack is preferable. Customize the carton, or cut it down if it becomes too heavy.

Fountains

There again, we have concrete to work with nine out of ten times. Let's hope yours breaks down into sections. If it's all one piece, and it weighs over a hundred pounds, your only choice is a sturdy wood crate. Anything else is a bad gamble. I have transported huge concrete, single piece fountains as is before, but I would never recommend it.

Bricks and concrete blocks

Cut down book cartons or wood boxes are your only hope for the bricks. Concrete blocks can be successfully transported without packing or wrapping. Bricks can too, if you can stand all the trips to and from the truck.

GARAGE ITEMS

CHAPTER THIRTY THREE

GARAGE ITEMS

If your garage is anything like the norm, you've probably stood in the doorway and wondered if and how you would ever work your way through the maze of clutter to the back wall. Or, perhaps you're one of those orderly types who regard the garage as your sacred sanctuary and deem it off limits to wife, children... and even car. You have everything under control and you know where every item is at all times.

Whichever you are, you've probably got some packing to do. The garage is about the only area of the home where your large trash cans and old wood boxes make suitable packing cartons.

Since there's no concern that your trash cans will be loaded any way but upright on the truck, you can fill them to the top with small tools, sports equipment, and any stray item lying about. Try not to leave anything protruding over the top rim of the can, bearing in mind that other items may be stacked on it when loading.

Once the trash cans are full, you can fill any old wood box that may be lying around. The heavier the items, the better, as wood doesn't give way and tear apart like cardboard cartons.

Next, you can turn to the packed cartons you may be storing. Check them to be certain the contents are secure, retape the cartons as necessary and mark the contents.

If there remains heavy items to pack and you have to turn to cardboard, use dish packs or medium cartons. Dish packs are the strong ones, and medium cartons are not too difficult to handle, even if they contain heavy weight.

Other items normally found in the garage such as: wicker baskets, drop cloths, rags, camping gear, small electrical items, and toys can usually be packed in large cartons.

Nuts, halts, nails, and screws should be packed in a book carton. If you happen to own a nuts and bolts cabinet (the plastic type with the little drawers), you had better tape the drawers shut. If you choose to go a step further, wrap and pack it in a carton.

Glassware of any type should always be packed.

Items like wagons, bikes, tricycles, strollers, scooters, sprayers, seeders, wet/dry vacuums, suitcases, backpacks, skis, and garden tools are all in the 'load as is' group and won't need to be wrapped or packed. Coolers and tool and tackle boxes are also in the 'load as is' group.

Reels, hooks, and line should be removed from fishing rods. Bundle the rods together and tape or tie at both ends. If your garage inventory includes trunks or footlockers, by all means, fill them up...or keep them ready for those last minute items. A footlocker or large trunk is usually much easier to locate when you're searching for those critical (unpack first) items at your destination.

After all, there isn't a carton made that's stronger than a trunk. If no trunk exists, remember to have enough cartons on hand for those last minute items.

Weights

If you're packing weights (as in weight lifting), use nothing larger than a book carton. Even at that, you must not fill the carton more than half full...unless you're superman. After filling it only half full, cut the corners of the carton down to the top of the contents, fold all the flaps over, and tape or tie the carton tightly. You're still apt to find yourself lifting almost one hundred and twenty pounds. Whatever you do, tape the carton bottom very securely.

As I complete the packing segment of this publication, I have, to my best recollection, covered every item generally found in the average home. Some will apply to you and some won't. However, every item I've ever packed throughout my career is mentioned herein. If you discover any item that isn't covered by the basics, or that I haven't mentioned, then chances are I've never handled it.

BE PREPARED

CHAPTER THIRTY FOUR

BE PREPARED

The moment you decide to move is the moment you should start preparing. Moving day is NOT the day to be taking down fixtures, discarding, disassembling furniture, or packing, except for the last minute items. If all is not ready when it's time to begin loading that truck, you could be in for the longest, most expensive day of your life.

If it takes more than an hour or so to complete the last minute chores, you could lose precious time. It's like cramming for a final exam, or the feeling you get when you're already late for work or an important appointment, and you're stuck in gridlock traffic.

Being unprepared can put you in a helter-skelter situation.
Helter + skelter + rush = accident = damage = expense.

If you're not accustomed to moving household goods or loading a truck, the job can exact a harsh toll on mind and body. To me, there's nothing worse than to be interrupted from loading the truck, only to have to complete some minor chore that could have and should have already been completed. I hate loose ends, particularly when I'm paying for labor to help me load.

DISASSEMBLE

CHAPTER THIRTY FIVE

DISASSEMBLE

What you are about to read is designed to save much needed space on the truck. It should also save you time in loading and costly repairs.

Keys

Breaking a key inside a cabinet or desk lock can be quite expensive. Losing one can be also. Always remove them from whatever item they service, desks, file cabinets, china cabinets, grandfather clocks, tool boxes, safes, antique cabinets, etc. I usually collect them all and consolidate them into one of a box of Ziploc bags I carry around in the truck.

If you should happen to own a metal four drawer file cabinet with the push to lock button located in the top front right corner of the cabinet, press to lock so that it doesn't catch the surface of another object...unless you don't have a key. If by chance you don't, tape tightly around the knob several times. This should cushion any blow to another item and prevent the lock from accidentally depressing.

China cabinet or hutch

Assuming it's a two piece item, move it a few inches away from the wall to allow you to disconnect and separate the top and bottom. After separation, disconnect and secure the electric cord (if applicable) and lower the top section onto the floor. Shrink wrap tightly around both sections. Be sure to cover the bottom corner.

Shrink wrapping should hold the glass tightly and keep it from rattling. It will also keep the base drawers and doors from opening and protect the finish.

Dining and kitchen table

One mistake often made is loading a table (any table) on it's legs in the truck. I guess the idea is to stuff items underneath and load bulky items on top of it... bad idea! The truck is in motion, the load shifts ever so slightly, putting additional pressure on the legs or base. The legs crack, come loose, or break. There are also additional problems in working a table around corners, down hallways, and through doorways with the legs attached. And finally, as you'll soon learn, it makes for a terribly wide tier.

To protect that beautiful, flawless dining table finish, there exists only one method to my liking. While it is still in the dining room and intact, drape a pad over the top and use a considerable amount of shrink wrap over the top and around the edges. When that's done, flip it upside down and remove the legs or base.

Shrink wrapping leather or vinyl

There are two fabrics to which stretch film or shrink wrap is harmful when directly applied. Those fabrics are leather and vinyl. We have been instructed not to shrink wrap either one because the fabrics sweat and could be permanently marked. However, there is a way around this problem. The key words here are direct application.

I have discovered that by first thoroughly wrapping the leather or vinyl item in cloth or paper pads, the way was then clear to apply the shrink wrap. I assume it has something to do with the pad absorbing whatever moisture develops. At any rate, the procedure has worked well for me.

High gloss veneer is another surface not suitable to direct application of shrink wrap.

Shrink wrap upholstery illustration

#1: If the sofa has a skirt, this must be wrapped first. Begin by tying the shrink wrap around one of the sofa legs.

Then flip the skirt up and begin making the first wrap around the sofa. Wrap the sofa as you walk around it, being careful to overlap each application by approximately 4 inches (Figure 1a). Continue in this manner until you reach the upper edge of the arm rests (Figure 1b).

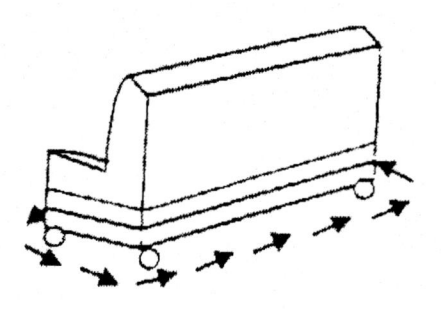

#2: Beginning at the front leg area of the sofa, shrink wrap the arm rest, overlapping both sides. Continue applying the film by covering the top ridge of the backrest, twisting the film while changing directions from the arm rest to the backrest. From the back, twist the film over the other arm rest and down to the edge of the front leg area of the sofa. (Figure 2)

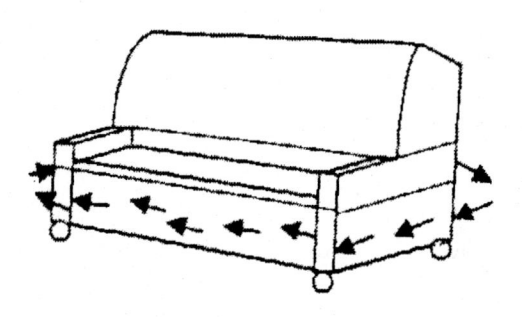

#3: Since the shrink wrap adheres to itself, you can now circle the entire sofa lengthwise, top to bottom. Use the same principal for overstuffed chairs and recliners.

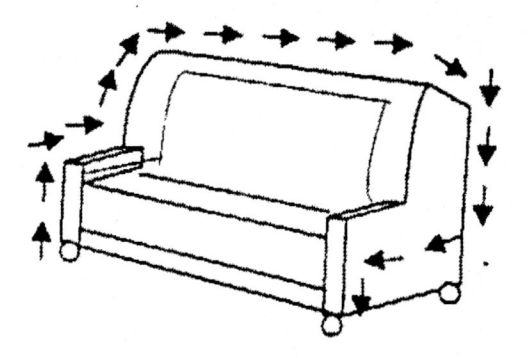

Recliner

Shrink wrapping will prevent the chair from suddenly bursting open as you lift it. It will also protect the side handle, as well as the fabric. Always wrap and load recliners in a closed position.

Hide-a-bed

Shrink wrapping this heavyweight is the order of the day. However, before you start wrapping, you'll have to make a decision...to leave or remove the inner mattress. Leaving it in adds more weight, but saves space. Removing it will cost you more work, it's your choice. Securing the bed frame to the sofa front cross piece to prevent it from flying open was once a must. However, I've discovered a shrink wrapping method that removes the need to tie it down. See illustration below.

First, shrink wrap lengthwise. Then stand hide-a-bed on end and shrink wrap again.

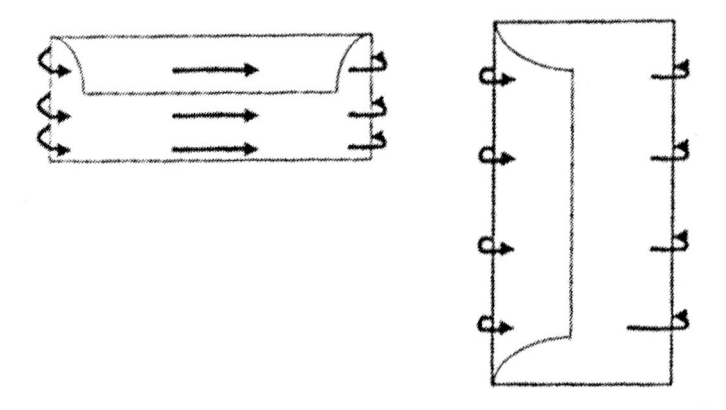

Trundle bed or Hollywood

Shrink wrap or carton pack the two mattresses. Flatten and secure the bottom spring in at least two places to prevent it snapping open. Disassemble the back and side pieces. Screws and bolts in the good ol' Ziploc bag.

Exercise equipment

I have frequently found it tedious working with some of the larger intricate pieces of equipment. It's very time consuming trying to disassemble a piece, only enough to save what little space you can in the truck Yet it must be done, if only to get it out the door. It's difficult to stack and a real challenge (for me) to reassemble, even with written directions.

It's also sometimes difficult to protect the on-board electronics without dismantling the piece all the way to scratch. I regret I cannot offer much advice, except to pack all loose items, store the nuts and bolts, fold whatever will fold, and pad it well. By all means, hang on to all written instructions.

Ironing board

Ironing board covers should be removed as should any loose rubber caps at the base, unless you'd care to wrap the works in a paper pad. Then, it'll be ready to load in the truck with no additional padding.

Headboard

All that is needed in preparing any size headboard for transit is to remove any protruding metal frame connection. This will prevent any possibility of gouging or scratching the item in front or behind it in the truck.

For those headboards with shelves and mirrors, if the mirror is not removable, shrink wrap the entire headboard.

Bed frames

I've always broken the metal ones down, folded and taped the moving parts, bundled them together, and wrapped them in a furniture or paper pad. Some frames require the removal of the casters before they can be folded. Bundling them saves lots of space. Don't forget the clips and casters.

You're probably wondering why I bother wrapping them since it's unlikely that they'll get scratched...even if they do, who cares? Good point! However, when loading, I might find a spot for them next to a dresser or an expensive sofa My reason for wrapping frames is not so much for the damage they might receive, as the damage they might cause.

Crib and play pen

Disassembling of a crib is always necessary, even if you have the folding type. Don't forget the bolts, screws, and springs. Tape the slide rods and the rail bar in one bundle. Pad wrap rails and crib ends. The mattress should be boxed or at least wrapped in a pad.

It seems I'm always removing little clamped gadgets from play pen side rails and cribs. I usually pack them and the play pen floor pad to keep it clean.

Toddler items

I guess car seats, highchairs, and bassinets would fall into this category. Nothing but pad wrapping needs to be done with these items. About all I've ever done to a musical swing is to fold and paper pad it.

Armoire

As I leap from the small items to the giant, I would advise shrink wrapping to keep swinging doors and drawers shut.

This is a difficult item to pad wrap if you're not equipped with large pads and big rubber bands. Be sure to check the legs before moving it. Some armoires I've seen can be dismantled into two or three pieces. I hope yours is one of those. Whatever you do, don't fill it with any other items to save space.

Drafting table

If possible, I've always removed the top to lighten the load and to protect the hinges and metal side gadgetry. I don't think it's a good idea to leave the top on and load on top of it. This could indent and warp the top.

Desk

Depending on the size, I've always emptied and packed the drawer contents in case it had to be flipped on end, or on it's side to fit through a doorway. Shrink wrap over all the drawers to prevent them opening suddenly. Actually shrink wrapping will save you pulling all the drawers and will also give you a little protection in case of a tight squeeze.

Shelves

Disassemble any kind of shelving that you can. Most I've handled take up lots of space is the truck and don't have the strength to hold much of anything in transit.

Coffee-end tables

Unscrew the legs and wrap them (if applicable). If the legs won't come off a coffee or end table, I've wrapped the table in a pad' making sure the legs were covered, flipped it upside down, and fitted a carton between the legs to square the package and to utilize the space.

Curio cabinet-glass case

I assume you've removed all the shelves and packed them. Shrink wrap from top to bottom. Follow the same procedure as you did with the china cabinet.

Entertainment center

Roll up and tape or tie any electrical cord. I usually shrink wrap over any doors or drawers. I have often reloaded the television in it's original slot after pad wrapping it, assuming it fit.

Small stereo cabinet

The glass door should be removed and packed. However, I've transported cabinets with glass intact and not had any problems, by shrink wrapping the entire cabinet very tightly and using extreme caution when loading. It must be kept upright with glass to the wall.

Tiered glass bookcase

This item seems to be popular enough to deserve mention. Do not try to move it intact. Disconnect the sections, remove and pack glass lids. The sections will have to be top-loaded.

Electrical cords

Have you ever unplugged a floor lamp or television and, while attempting to move the item, caught the cord or stepped on it? If so, I hope you were fortunate not to injure yourself, or snap the plug off the cord. In the course of your move, you'll be unplugging and plugging those same items a couple of times. When you first unplug the item, take the time to roll and secure that dangling cord.

Built-ins

I could write you pages of horror stories on this subject, but I know you're busy so I'll keep this story short.

When Mr. C moved into his present home, he chose one of the bedrooms for his office. His desk, computer, and file cabinet fit perfectly. However, he had a library of text books and no place to store them.

Carpenters came to his home, and in one day, built and installed beautiful wall to wall, floor to ceiling bookcases on the spot. Now, he's planning a move and he intends to include those bookcases. He never gave a thought to moving them out...until it was time to load them. Suddenly, he discovered they wouldn't fit through the door. He tried wishing them out, but God wouldn't listen. He still had choices. He could pull them away from the wall and dismantle them, and probably tear up the walls in the process. Or, he could leave them. What's your choice?

Refrigerator-freezer food

When you last vacationed or went on holiday, you probably did one of three things. You took most of the food along in your cooler, you stuffed yourselves before leaving to prevent waste, or in planning ahead, you let the inventory run down to bare necessity. Then again, maybe you gave the food away, or simply tossed it. Now that you're moving, the above choices will probably be the same, with one exception. It won't be a vacation or a holiday.

If you're moving around the corner or across town, chances are you won't have to dispose of anything. If you're planning a short move (a day or so), leave the frozen foods in place, but empty the ice trays and remove all breakables. Under normal conditions, a freezer full of frozen food should take about eighteen hours to thaw once the plug is pulled. First rule: Leave nothing in the refrigerator section, no matter what the distance.

If the move involves any distance or time over eighteen hours, I suggest you also empty the freezer. When you do, grab an old sock, fill it about halfway with fresh coffee grounds. Then, hang or place a sock in each of the refrigerator or freezer compartments. This will help prevent mildew and neutralize terrible odors.

Always remove all magnetized items from the doors. Second rule: Do not fill the freezer or refrigerator with foreign objects to save space. It could be the costliest mistake you've ever made.

Microwave oven

Load right side up and pad well. Don't load too much weight on the top.

Washer

I always totally disconnect both water hoses and drain bose. I wrap them in paper and store them inside the washer. Washer packs are used to secure the inside tub. If not at your truck rental agency, they're available at local moving companies and appliance stores. Check your machine instruction booklet. Some of the newer models don't require the package. Be sure to secure the electric cord.

Dryer

Disconnect the air duct hose completely, clamps, and all. Shake the loose lint out, paper wrap, and store in tub. Secure the electric cord, or if yours is gas operated, be sure to cap the outlet, and totally remove the gas line.

Air condition-humidifier

Nothing to do with these except pad well. Be sure the humidifier tub is dry.

Playhouse-castle-cabin, etc,

If they can't be dismantled, I hope you reserved a very large truck. The plastic ones take only a little pounding with a rubber mallet.

Swing set

There's not much I can tell you that you don't already know. Don't lose the nuts and bolts. Don't wait too long to think about loading that long top swing set bar on moving day.

Barbecue

Empty used charcoal and wipe down or hose off. If yours is butane or gas, disconnect the tank. I believe butane tanks can be traded for empties. Inquire.

Insurance regulations prohibit the transportation of butane tanks by the moving industry. If you're thinking of taking the gamble, ask yourself if the sum total of your household goods equals the fifteen or so dollars you'll save on replacement.

Garden hose

Whether your hose is wound up in a reel or naked in the grass, connecting both ends will save a messy leak.

Table saw-machinery

If your inventory includes this item and any type of saw or drill press or machinery, I'm certain you know better than I do how to secure them. My sole purpose in bringing them to light, was to remind myself that eventually these items will have to be loaded and that my advice may be necessary.

Bicycles

Some of the newer racing bikes come completely apart with the turn of a couple of knobs. Then, there are the older models that you can condense in size by unscrewing the pedals and turning the handlebars. And finally, there are the customized mountain bikes that have stationary, high tech handlebars and pedals that are form fitted to your feet. Tampering with the third group can ruin the intricate balance of the bike and probably get you one to five at Leavenworth.

The only advice I can give on the matter is, if you're cramped for space on the truck and your bike fits the category of groups one or two...go for it! When you remove the pedals and turn the handlebars, the bike becomes much slimmer, about the thickness of a mattress and much easier to load.

Fuel burning lawn equipment

This applies to mowers, edge tools, trimmers, power saws, etc. Always remove fuel for obvious reasons. Gasoline is highly flammable. I'll add one other reason....spillage. Inside the van, even if it doesn't ignite, spillage can be costly. Besides soaking whatever items are around the spill, the fumes can seep into upholstery and linens and remain there forever.

Also, be sure to load each of this type item upright to prevent oil seepage.

Greasy-oily items

If your hobby happens to be overhauling engines or transmissions, or tinkering with some kind of motor, chances are you're concerned about how to handle some of the greasy-oily parts. Maybe your power mower or edge tool is throwing oil, or your barbecue is a mess.

You've already read how shrink wrap protects an item from outside dirt and dust. It can also work in reverse. Shrink wrap can lock in that grease and oil and prevent it from ruining anything it might come in contact with, such as your hands, clothes, and the pad you use to cover the item with. It works for me.

This will conclude the disassembling segment of this publication. You must have noticed my enthusiasm for shrink wrap and the many new uses I have discovered, besides upholstery protection. It has eliminated many concerns I once had in the handling of household goods, and made my work so much simpler. It will for you also.

APPLIANCE DOLLY

CHAPTER THIRTY SIX

APPLIANCE DOLLY

What would one do without the appliance dolly? My answer to that is "break our backs"! Seriously, it is one of the greatest labor saving devices ever invented. However, if used improperly, it can hurt you and can cost you money. For now, I'll skip the 'hurt yous' and go right to the 'cost you monies'.

#1 A dolly used on carpeted stairways can leave belt marks.
#2 Turning a loaded dolly in a tight area can gouge a big hole in a wall or door.
#3 Dropping down over brick steps can chip the edges.
#4 Dragging an appliance dolly over uneven terrain, gravel, or loose dirt can cause your appliance to suddenly flip over.
#5 If you can't see where you're going when pushing an appliance, get help.
#6 When hooking up to a refrigerator or upright freezer, be certain the dolly is on the door handle side of the appliance. This will prevent any doors from swinging open.

Furniture pads

The furniture pad is vital to the survival of your household goods. I realize that they cost extra when renting a truck, but consider the damage an unprotected dresser or china cabinet could encounter. Padded items afford you more options in the placing of items when loading a truck, than unpadded items do. No matter how careful you are in moving an item, without covering that item with a pad, you're sentencing it to probable death or serious injury.

If you followed the advice regarding the use of paper pads and shrink wrap, chances are you'll have reduced the need of the rental pads by a considerable amount.

LOADING THE TRUCK

CHAPTER THIRTY SEVEN

LOADING THE TRUCK

You are about to enter the point of no return...the blood and guts portion of the move. Everything you own is packed in a carton, stuffed in a drawer, shrink wrapped, or wrapped in a paper pad. The coffee pot is gone, leaving you with no excuse whatsoever to be standing around. To settle the butterflies in your stomach, you tour the war zone one last time. Then, you stand in your driveway or behind the truck, stare inside at the dark gaping hole, and ask yourself, "What if I can't get it all in?"

I've got news for you. Last year alone I hauled seventy six shipments, including eleven cars, and I'll bet I asked myself that same question over a half dozen times.

Picture the inside dimensions of the van as a three dimensional puzzle board, and imagine each item as a puzzle piece. At this point, you must realize that without surveying your particular inventory or knowing the size and contents of your job, that I cannot advise on where and how to place each item. I will attempt to cover all the basics and to point out certain aspects and ramifications. Hopefully, relevant to your particular situation.

As I sit at my desk pondering what to write next, I Almost wish I were there to help you load the truck. I think it would be easier than sitting here trying to write out advice.

Let's start loading the first tier. For your purposes, a tier will be a single stack of various items from wall to wall, and floor to ceiling.

One of your objectives here will be to try to keep the tiers even. The wall you are stacking against will already insure one side being even. It will be your duty to see that the backside ends up the same way. I will not mention padding on the assumption that you are already handling that chore.

I have always begun my first tier with flat items against the wall, picture cartons, crib rails and sides, headboards, table tops, etc. These are good items to dispose of immediately as they don't stand up on their own and seem to take up lots of room when leaning against a wall. By placing them up front and between the tiers, they don't need to be tied off, secured, or held up, except by the tier behind them.

Directly behind these flat items, I'd load the heaviest dresser, highboy chest, small desk, or file cabinet...any heavy item with a common approximate depth. Let's assume you have a dresser and highboy chest side by side as base. If these items don't take up all the wall to wall space, calculate how much floor space you have left and choose a heavy item that might fit. It could be a book carton, a dish pack, or a footlocker.

Once you've filled that wall to wall space, you're ready to start up the mountain with the second layer. Try to remember as many items in your inventory as you can. Difficult as this might be, you can simplify that in two ways. First, by grouping certain items together according to size, such as night stands, end tables, two drawer filing cabinets, microwave ovens, medium and large cartons, and kitchen chairs. Yes, kitchen chairs. Place a kitchen chair next to a medium carton. If you removed the back of the chair and left just the seat and legs, you could see that the overall dimensions are very close. So you set a medium carton on a dresser, pad a kitchen chair, and kneel it over the carton. Or, lay the chair on it's back next to the carton, and your tier is even................... another piece to the puzzle solved.

The second way to keep track of your inventory, is by taking quick tours each time you walk in to retrieve a particular item. The smaller the job, the less your memory will have to be jogged.

There's one thing you'll learn immediately when loading the truck. The heavier the object, the closer to the floor you must load it. I believe that will come naturally to you.

Okay, you've put away two night stands, a microwave oven, and two medium cartons on top of the base items. It's time to load some lighter items, chairs, lighter medium cartons, lamp tables, a couple of plastic toys, maybe a doll house or cooler.

You've stacked three layers of items on the base and you still have a three to five inch gap to the ceiling. Small step ladders, garden tools, folding chairs, small bundled items, fishing rods, throw rugs, table legs, ironing boards, make for great top fillers as long as nothing is too heavy. Remember, you are stacking atop chairs, lamp tables, plastic toys, and the like.

Your first tier is now complete. The load is tight with no empty spaces and the tier is even. You managed to dispose of three wood shelves underneath the dresser, and every item is padded and well protected. Take a break and then another tour.

Following your break, halfway through your survey, you've discovered a problem. There lies the top bar of the swing set in the back yard. You can see that it won't stand upright in the truck. Nor will it fit across. It's fifteen feet long. Lengthwise is the only answer. You're fortunate to have discovered it in time. You still have space enough.

Whenever I encounter an over length item, I usually secure it in one of the high corners of the van. This puts it out of harm's way and I don't have to fight it, except when top loading.

With that out of the way, let's load a tier of upholstery. I prefer to load the largest sofa first, on end, back to the load, legs to the side wall. I load the next one on the opposite wall, and the love seats, recliners, and chairs in the middle. If you don't have enough upholstery to complete a tier, refer to the grouping of similar sized objects, such as a rocker, extra large cartons, patio chairs, chaise-lounges, ottomans, or a bulky item to replace one of the long sofas as base. Think about a couple of tall bookcases, which, standing back to back, nearly match the space taken up by a sofa. A refrigerator, washer, or dryer could also work.

There are an infinite number of possibilities. Two dish packs side by side and two deep are also the approximate depth of a sofa. A vivid imagination and an open mind will be extremely handy.

Other unlikely partners, the table saw and refrigerator can ride side by side with no problem. Others are the workbench, the washer, the bookcase, and the hutch top. Or stranger yet, the upright piano and the wardrobe.

To mention a few never do's:

Never load the face of a glass front cabinet anywhere near a protruding object.

Never load bare wood against cardboard.

Finally, never load a carton on it's side...unless it's bedding, clothing, or linens.

There are thousands of quality household goods packers and movers in the business and I'll bet my last dollar that not any two would load your shipment the same exact way. As a matter of fact, given the same shipment to load a half dozen times, I'll wager I wouldn't load every item in exactly the same spot.

Throughout this publication, I have given you all that has worked well for me time and time again.

ILLUSTRATION #1

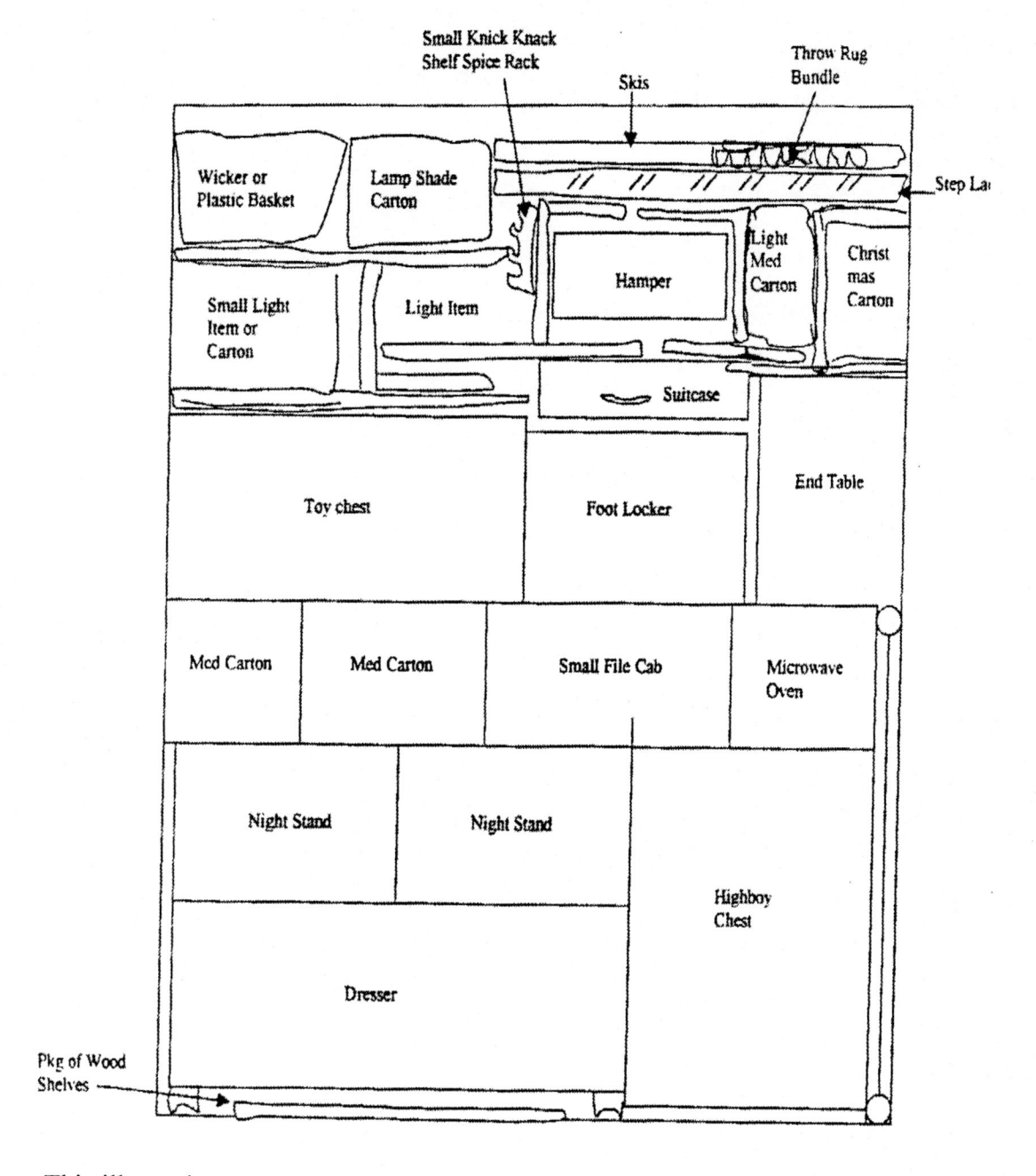

This illustration represents a typical tier. They won't all be this square and this simple, but it's a start.

109

ILLUSTRATION # 2

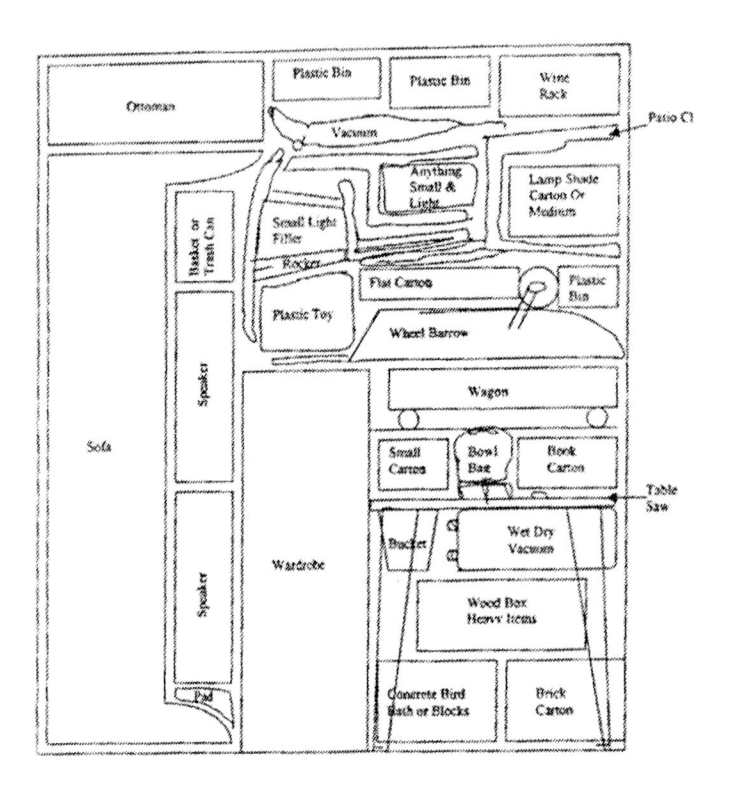

This illustration is primarily aimed at loading the sofa and odd strapped items – table saw, wheelbarrow, and rocker.

ILLUSTRATION # 3

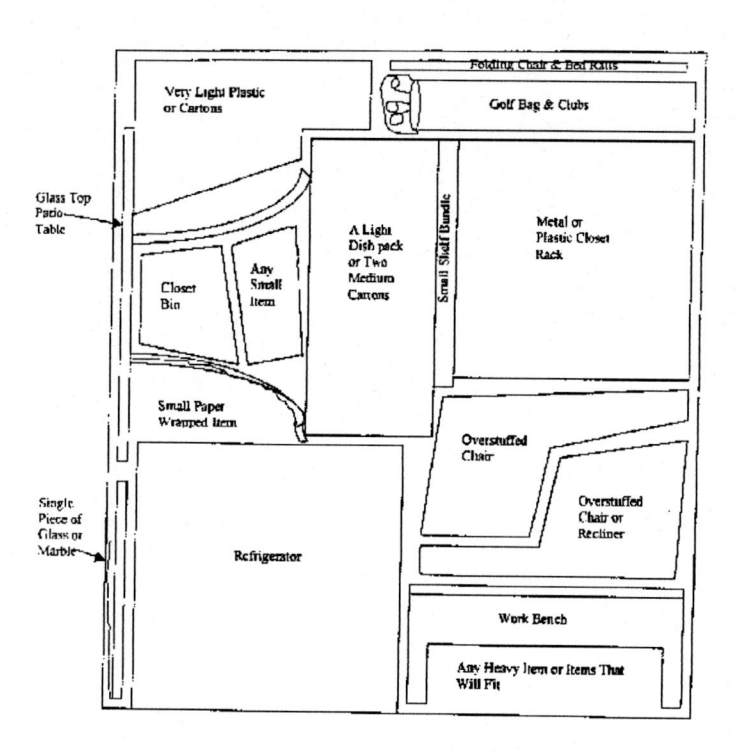

This illustration points out how I dispose of overstuffed furniture and, of course, the glass top patio table.

ILLUSTRATION # 4

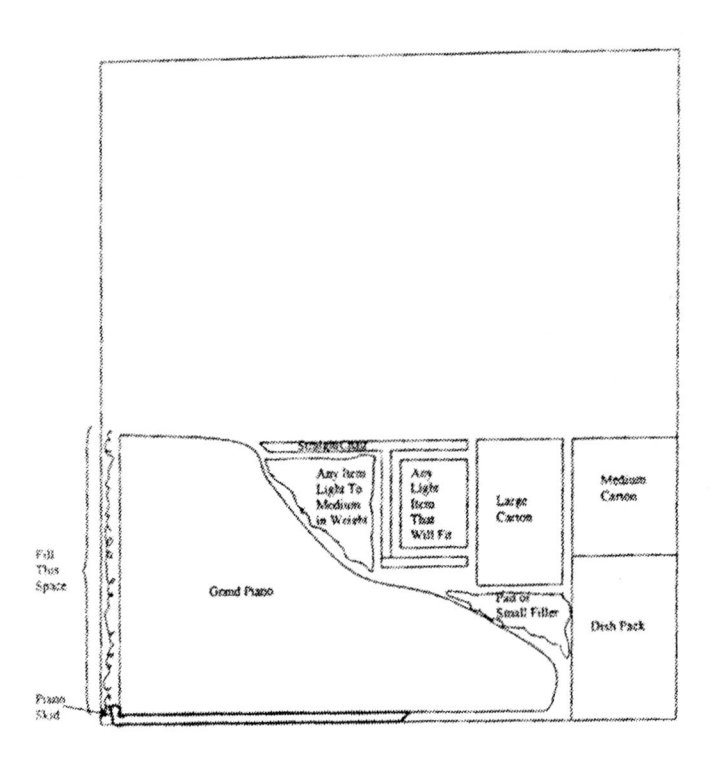

Grand Piano illustration

FURNITURE HANDLING

CHAPTER THIRTY EIGHT

FURNITURE HANDLING

Successful furniture handling is an art. By successful, I mean two or three people working together as a team that can move about every heavy, awkward, cumbersome item from any room in the house, through doorways, down halls, around corners, and up and down stairways without sustaining any damage to the item, the surrounding property (walls and rails) or themselves. 'Practice makes perfect' certainly applies to this line of business.

When I'm working near home, I use the same contract labor as I have for years. We reached a point years ago where they can almost read my mind. I often find as I'm thinking about the next item I want to load, they are walking or wheeling it toward the truck.

Lifting and carrying a heavy item, for us, is like a marine corps drill. We're almost in perfect harmony as we march down the hallway. When one of us has to raise or lower the object in preparation for a tight turn, the other reacts instantly and smoothly with balance or a counter move. I miss this harmony when I'm on the road and forced to hire contract labor that I've never worked with. Strangers on the other end of a heavy object can hurt you.

When you see a bulky item that looks like it could be trouble, stop, make a plan, and add a contingency. Make the guy on the other end aware of your plan before you touch the item. Lift with your legs and not your back, and lift together. If you're moving up or down a set of stairs, drape a pad over the stair railings or the item in case of a slip. If a dresser is too heavy, pull the drawers. Carry the shell to the truck and reinsert the drawers there.

When you're fighting a bulky item through a narrow doorway, or making a tight turn, watch your knuckles. Mine are laden with battle scars.

Long items

Please don't think I'm trying to insult anyone's intelligence, but since I've been witness to what I'm about to write, I thought it best to mention. To illustrate my point, I'll use the name 'Ralphy' and get real graphic.

Ralphy strolls to the master bedroom to retrieve two large water bed rails. As he's hoisting the two long pieces upon his shoulder, he snaps three of five ceiling fan blades. As he ambles through the doorway and turns down the hall, the metal edge of his bundle tears through a chunk of doorjamb. Peeking over his shoulder to glance at the doorjamb, he inadvertently shears off a hall wall light with the front of his bundle. As he makes his final turn to exit the house, the glass shade from a hanging lamp in the foyer bites the dust.

Only parts of this story are true. I made up the rest. When you're handling a long item, be certain you're in control of both ends at all times.

Sliding appliance

No, it's not a new gadget. It's about moving an appliance across linoleum or tile. Never attempt to slide any heavy appliance across a linoleum or tiled surface without first slipping a pad between the casters or wheels and the floor surface. In all honesty, I must confess that I have committed this crime twice. The first time, I gouged a seven inch section of linoleum when I attempted to slide a refrigerator out of it's cranny. The second was with a washer that broke two tiles and cracked a third. The first accident cost me $87.00 and the second $112.50.

Bulky sofa

When it's time to load the sofa or love seat, I've found it easiest to handle when carrying it in a kneeling position (back to the ceiling-front to the floor). It seems easier to maneuver when making a turn, and also easier to grip, particularly if it's been shrink wrapped.

Mattress-overhead

Mattresses should be fairly easy items to move. They're thin in comparison to a dresser, therefore can slip through a doorway and down the narrowest of hallways with ease. They're simple to load on a truck and can be used to hold and tie off a load.

They can also destroy a ceiling fan or smoke alarm in an instant, and can shatter a light fixture without hesitation. The advice offered here is to be aware of the overhead.

PIANOS

CHAPTER THIRTY NINE

PIANOS

If you're an average guy with no prior moving experience, then I strongly suggest you phone any number of piano movers in the phone book. For a nominal fee, they will come to your home, load the piano on the truck, and make it look easy in the process. They also have the proper equipment which, if you undertake to do yourself, would still cost you to rent. Have I convinced you yet? Your budget's depleted and you don't have the time.

Let's start with the Spinet...the smallest of the brutes. Remove the music holder, lift the piano, and center it upright on a four wheeled dolly. It's ready.

Now, for the upright piano. One or two persons lift only one end of the piano high enough to slip a four wheeled dolly under the center. Once the dolly is placed, let the piano back down slowly and gently. Be careful not to allow the dolly to slip out from the bottom. The piano is down, centered on the dolly, and it's stable. It's ready.

"Are you Okay?", I always ask members of my crew as I watch the protruding veins in their necks shrink back to normal.

Next we'll tackle the group of pianos known as the 'Grands'. These little monsters will require three men for weight and balance, a piano sled or skid, a rubber mallet, a large standard screw driver, and a four wheeled dolly.

You might be able to rent or borrow a sled or skid from a moving company, just to get the piano on and off the truck. The piano can ride on pads while it's in transit. Assuming the manpower and equipment are all lined up, let's get started.

Never place a Spinet or Upright piano totally on end. Unlike the Grands, the keyboards and innards are not built to withstand this type of punishment. If you try it, you might get lucky, but what are the odds?

When rolling a piano even on a proper dolly, always be certain there is someone on each end. Dollies can run away or come to a sudden halt and dump a piano.

Stairs

This is where the nightmare becomes all too real. Where the war begins is between brute force and the immovable object. Even as I write, my body stiffens and the adrenalin begins to flow. If you're unfortunate to have stairs, utilize the truck ramp or walk board if you can. If that won't work, then I'll remind you once again of the phone book and the piano movers.

Before you start down, do a quick survey for broken or uneven steps, turns, or curves. Make sure the back of the piano is against any inside curve. If things get a little tight, and an accident should occur, you'll dent or scratch the rear of the piano, and not the front. If there are railings, drape a blanket or pad over them, particularly on the corners or turns.

Remove the dolly before you start down the stairs, as it now becomes a liability. You'll need the strongest, most knowledgeable people on the bottom end of the piano. The person on the top will have some lifting and holding back to do, as well as guiding the piece. On the backside of almost every Spinet and Upright piano, there's a handgrip that sets approximately halfway down between two pieces of framework. Become familiar with it immediately. It is vital to the success of this piano move.

Once you start down, the sheer weight and casters will probably cause a halt as it catches each step. You'll have to lift the whole piano just enough to clear the edge of each step so as not to damage the stairs or the corners of the piano. Drop one step at a time and set the piano back down. It's simply a matter of repetition all the way to the bottom. Once you've reached the bottom, place it back on the dolly and pat yourself on the back.

Grand piano-stairs

The piano sled or skid will make a world of difference in that it will almost slide down the stairs by itself, every time you lift. The key here will be to hold it back. Again, move one or two steps at a time and be careful not to tip it to either side. Be certain the keyboard end of the piano (barrier end of the sled) is on the bottom when you start down.

LOAD A PREVIOUSLY DAMAGED ITEM

CHAPTER FORTY

LOAD A PREVIOUSLY DAMAGED ITEM

Let's assume that you have a large cabinet, highboy chest, or a cedar chest that is fairly heavy with loaded drawers and a broken leg. It's an heirloom. The leg can and will be repaired some day, but not before moving day. I've illustrated two ways in which this particular item can be loaded safely, without sustaining any further damage.

Be certain the contents are secure before laying any item on it's side or on end.

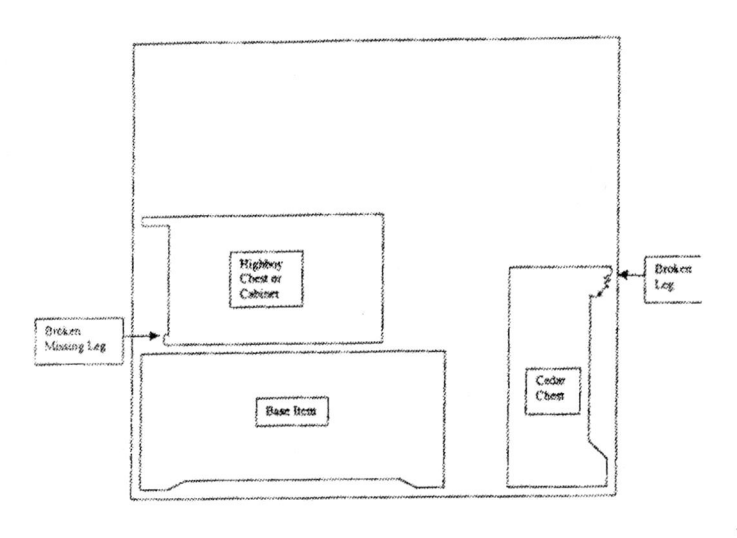

Illustration #1

Illustration #2

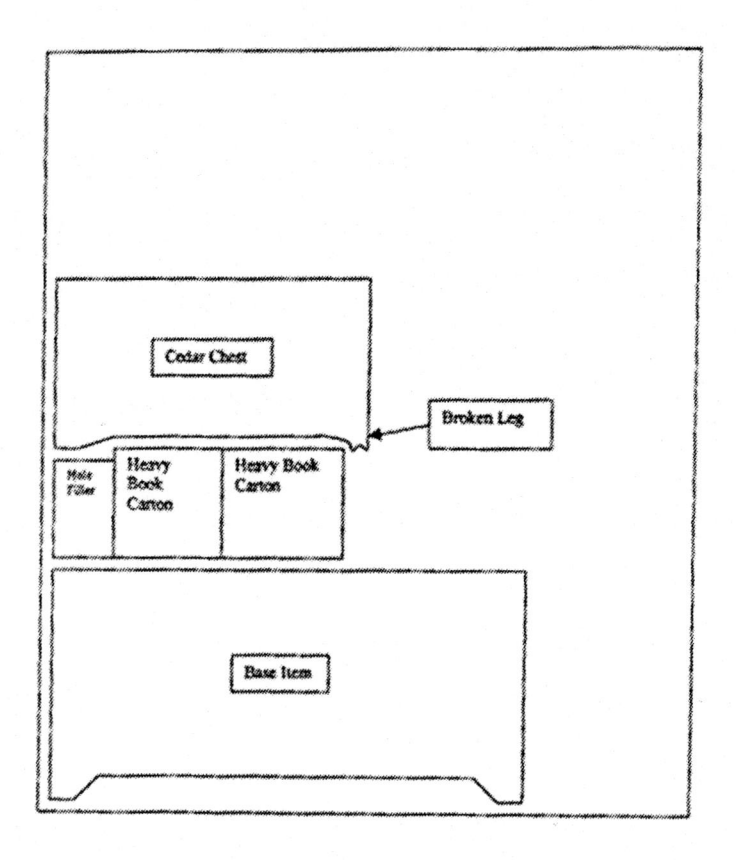

You could use the same technique for any chest or cabinet as I did with the cedar chest.

SELF STORAGE

CHAPTER FORTY ONE

SELF STORAGE

If you're planning to store your goods in a self storage compartment, you may want to follow the truck loading guidelines and illustrations. Obviously, your tiers won't be as high as in the truck, but you'll be using the same basic principle.

If you require access to any of your goods from time to time, then you'll change the pattern of loading to allow yourself a pathway down the center of the compartment. I suggest loading the first tier against the back wall, the other two tiers against the side walls, and working your way out from there.

Since you'll be returning the truck and pads at some point, rather than storing bare furniture, try cardboard pieces over the base furniture, and paper pads over the remaining items. As long as your furniture is stationary, you needn't be concerned with rubbing or chafing.

COLD WEATHER

CHAPTER FORTY TWO

COLD WEATHER

This only concerns those of you whose destination is where the temperature dips to freezing or lower. This segment concerns your electrical items such as televisions, stereos, refrigerators, freezers, etc. And only if these items have sat in the truck long enough to take in the cold temperatures.

I don't claim to understand the technical intricacies of a TV or appliance, but I've heard that plugging in a television fresh off a cold truck can cause severe damage. Insurance companies have instructed us to advise the customer to hold off using any of these items until they have returned to room temperature, usually about twenty four hours. You may want to research this warning on your own.

KEEP PACK MATERIALS

CHAPTER FORTY THREE

KEEP PACKING MATERIALS

I've lived in the same house for twelve years. My neighbors only need to look around the corner to know if I'm in town, by the presence or absence of my truck.

I'm forever being asked if I have one, two, or a dozen empty cartons of one size or another. It occurs so often, that I've begun to keep an inventory of assorted used cartons in my garage.

My son pesters me at least half a dozen times a year to build him this or that from the larger cartons, and my relatives are always shipping something off to somebody. I frequently have a use for some of the smaller cartons, especially at Christmas time. The paper pads are also invaluable.

I guarantee if you want to make the entire block of neighbors your friends for life, let it be known you're storing an inventory of empty cartons.

About the Author

I began my career in the relocation industry in 1969 as an apprentice helper with a local Mayflower agency in Santa Monica, California. Within six months, I achieved local driver status and began training as a packer in both a local and long distance capacity. My eleven years with the agency included local and long distance packing, warehousing, local intrastate and interstate moving, driver foremanship and transcontinental relocating.

In the spring of 1981, I joined Global Van Lines as an owner-operator with the transcontinental fleet where I continued to practice all that I had I learned previously.

In 1988, following a brief illness, I took a job as a mover trainer to work with aspiring owner-operators. A year later, I rejoined the relocation ranks as a contract operator with Beverly Hills Transfer Company, an agent of Allied Van Lines. I also held a packing contract with the firm of more than three years where I supervised my own crews. While at Beverly Hills Transfer, I became involved with specific contracts connected with the relocation of Mariott Hotel executives that included the full-service package from origin to destination.

The desire to remain closer to home and family caused me to terminate an enjoyable contract with a Houston, Texas agency affiliated with Suddath United Van Lines. There again, I was involved with large corporate full-service relocation for such companies as Home-Express, the Bechtel Corporation, Texaco and Union Oil Companies, and the then "Houston Oilers" football team. I have handled countless military and C.O.D. relocations and also serviced a variety of international customers.

I am currently maintaining my ties to the industry as a contractor with a Wheaton Van Lines agency in Brea, California.